His Robe

Or Mine

FRANK B. PHILLIPS

Information other languages or on how to get additional
copies may be obtained by contacting
Justified Walk Ministries at
(269) 471-9224

Additional information about this book, sermon series,
and other resources by, or recommended by,
Frank B. Phillips
are listed at the end of this book, and on the internet at
www.justifiedwalk.com
or email us
justifiedwalk@justifiedwalk.com

All Scripture quotations are from the King James Version
unless otherwise noted. All other quotations, unless
otherwise noted, come from the writings of Ellen White.

Cover design by Jessica Schultz

Published by Justified Walk Ministries
PO Box 233
Berrien Springs, Michigan 49103-0233

This book is not for sale. It was paid for at the cross! In
light of the lateness of the hour and the urgency of the message contained, we are attempting to distribute this book as
broadly and as quickly as we possibly can. If you have been
blessed by what you have read, we pray that you will share
the book with someone else, and we will happily supply
additional copies. Donations to support this effort are grate-
fully accepted should the Lord put a burden on your heart
for such a donation. They are also tax deductible.

"Freely have ye received; freely give."
"It is in giving that we receive."

TABLE OF CONTENTS

Foreword

This book was written by the late Frank B. Phillips during a ten year period of His retirement years when he and his wife Dorothy were presenting the marvelous message of "Christ our Righteousness" in revival meetings. God greatly blessed his efforts. His sermons were eagerly listened to and rejoiced over, shared with others, and attendees experienced reviving renewal in their lives. In 1978 a week of prayer was held at Andrews University, during which Pastor Phillips was encouraged to prepare a manuscript for publication. He wrote the requested manuscript, but it unfortunately remained unpublished—almost forgotten—for more than twenty years.

Recently, however, through simple but wonderfully providential means, Elder Phillips' messages have been again brought to the attention of God's children—through the sharing of his revival sermons on cassettes, CDs, the internet, and now via this manuscript—and we are happy to report that God is using these messages in the same wonderful way again! We believe God has revived these messages to meet the urgent needs of His people who, in too many cases, have never personally heard or applied the life-changing truths of Christ Our Righteousness, and as a result have only minimally experienced the more abundant life anticipated in God's word.

We are accordingly pleased to provide his messages in this written form, and pray the assimilation of these truths will bring about that abundant life, and will allow each reader to become God's own fortress in this rebel world, each heart a strong tower for truth and love, and each life a beacon of light on a hill bringing others to the knowledge

The Wedding Garment
THE INTRODUCTION

The parable of the wedding garment holds a particular interest for God's people today. It, along with the parable of the ten virgins, has never been completed. In both cases the end of the parable does not occur until Jesus receives His bride. In the first parable the Groom is waiting for the bride. In the second, the bride is waiting for the Groom.

The wedding, itself, represents the union of humanity with divinity. The wedding garment, that must be worn, represents the character of Christ, which is an essential for each guest attending the marriage if they are to be accepted by the Father as the Groom's bride.

Matthew 22 pictures three separate occasions when the King, the Groom's Father, sent His servants out to bring the bride in for the wedding. The bride had been chosen and she had been informed and knew she was to be married to the Groom. The record reads, "He came unto his own, and his own received him not." John 1:11. The church, His chosen bride, was too busy and did not wish to consummate the marriage on the terms required by the Groom.

The problem was the wedding garment. The bride had insisted upon wearing a garment of her own choice—not that plain, old-fashioned garment which the Groom's Father had planned for her to wear.

The bride finally became so angered about the whole plan that she decided the only way out was to get rid of the Groom. In order for her to do this it was necessary for her to take full legal responsibility for the deed. There was a trial and, even though the judge and mob knew that the Groom was innocent, a great cry was heard from the bride, ". . . Away with him, away with him, crucify him." John 19:15. So the terrible deed was done. The sense of relief to the bride was short-lived, however, for the words of the Groom, spoken many days before, began to trouble her: ". . . Destroy this temple, and in three days I will raise it up." John 2:19. The bride remembered how many miracles He had performed when alive and her fear knew no bounds.

True to His word, the Groom returned on the third day—alive and well. He told one of the members of the bride's party that He must make a quick trip to see His Father to make sure that everything was all right as far as His own efforts to carry out His Father's plan were concerned. John 20:17.

The trip was made and on the same day He was back visiting with some of the members of the bride's family. This visit caused many of the bridal party to think very seriously. Could this be the same person that was crucified three days before? Finally, they were convinced that He was, indeed, the same person. The Groom's joy was great at being recognized, and He sent the whole group out to find the rest of the bridal party and bring them back to Him. The bride, however, had other ideas and refused to come. It was that wedding garment problem again.

The root of the problem was that every single member of the bride's party (the church) who had ever claimed to believe and accept the Groom had received a wedding garment. The question was not where to purchase one or how to make one, for when they accepted the invitation to become a member of the bride's party the garment was received as a gift. The problem was wearing it!

Now there came a time quite soon after this when the Groom saw that He was not going to be married to His chosen bride, for she refused to wear the garment. He, therefore, told His friends to stop trying to convince His chosen

bride to come and accept Him. He told them to go anywhere and find Him a bride that would be willing to wear
the garment.

They traveled far and wide. In fact, they went over the
"face of the whole earth" to carry the gospel (the good news)
giving the invitation (Colossians 1:23), but not many were
interested.

For the next (approximately) eighteen hundred years
many servants were sent out to represent the Groom and to
invite anyone to join the bridal party. It seemed the old
question kept coming up— the wedding garment. Some
said that it was not necessary to be so rigid. Some felt that
their own garment was good enough. The arguments went
on and on.

The time came when even the servants, themselves, were
confused. They were inviting the guests without even men-
tioning the garment that was necessary to be worn. Some
even said, "If you give enough money, you won't need to
worry about the garment." There were many who said, "We
are not sure what the garment is all about anyway, so just
forget it; only believe and you will be welcomed by the
Groom."

The years rolled by and the bride was still not ready. The
Groom was anxious to come and receive His bride so He
sent special instructions through one member of the bride's
party. He had often sent special instruction to His bride by
special messengers and, again, He hoped to clear away some
of the problems that had been so confusing by using this special gift. In these messages He was careful to give more
detailed instructions as to how to put on and wear the garment that seemed such a problem. The special instructions
were welcomed by some and rejected by others. Those who
accepted the added help seemed to get along well with the
garment in question. They found it a real blessing that solved
all of their problems. Those who rejected the help seemed
to still have the same old difficulties.

In time the King knew that He could not put the wedding off much longer. Therefore, He impressed Elders Jones and Waggoner in November of 1888 to meet with a part of the bridal party who were in conference studying how best to prepare the bride for the wedding. These two men insisted that the message they were preaching was the true way to get ready for the wedding.

The wedding garment was the problem again. Some were willing to wear part of the garment if they could adjust it to blend with their own. Others said they wanted no part of it at all. A few saw the garment as a gift and accepted it, wearing it gladly ever after.

The problem was not settled, however, as far as the bride was concerned. In a few years the problem seemed to go away. Another effort was made by the Groom to awaken His bride from her deadly slumber. This occurred in the early part of this century. Books were written and sent out with clear instructions as to how to get ready for the wedding. The bride, however, was still not sure about the garment, even though the Groom had continuously kept calling to her, "Awake, awake; put on thy strength, O Zion; put on thy beautiful garments . . ." Isaiah 52:1.

In patience the Groom waited until He could scarcely wait longer. Problems in the world were mounting so rapidly. Politically, economically, socially, environmentally, spiritually and physically the world had been brought to the brink of disaster. Once again the Groom has set Himself to prepare His bride to be ready for His soon return by urging them to be willing to wear the garment.

There is no garment like the wedding garment in the whole world. It brings peace, joy, satisfaction and love into the human heart. But it is invisible to the wearer, as well as to other members of the bridal party (the church). However, it becomes the magnetic force to draw others to accept the gospel invitation.

This is the reason that it was only when the King came in to see the guests at the wedding that the one not having on the wedding garment was speechless when asked about it. Matthew 22:12. He felt at home with the party until the King came in. Only then did he realize his pretense was recognized, and he was without excuse. Remember, he had received a garment when he accepted the invitation. What could he say? There, across his lap, was the garment neatly folded. He believed the principles it represented, but it was so uncomfortable to wear, it was so restricting. He intended to put it on and wear it, but not yet. No wonder he was speechless.

This book is intended to clearly reveal how to receive and wear the wedding garment which all must have and wear if they are to meet the Lord in peace and not be speechless when He comes. As you read the next chapter you will discover who is behind all this confusion and how you may be free from his power. Then, and only then, can we see clearly the "how" and "why" of God's great plan of redemption.

The companion CD that came with this book was a sermon by Frank Phillips entitled "How Good is Perfect". Please listen to the CD before reading the rest of the book. It will illustrate the principles of the book in a real life situation. If you did not receive one please give us a **call** at Justified Walk Ministries **(269) 471-9224** or **download** the #3 File of the Justified Walk Series off our website: **www. justifiedwalk.com** or email; justifiedwalk @justifiedwalk.com all materials are free of charge and will be shipped without fee.

1.

CONFIDENTIAL!
Top Secret Information!

The human mind is the battleground for the most deadly conflict ever fought on this planet. Christ seeks to control our minds so that we might reach the highest fulfillment of the capabilities that He, Himself, built into that marvelous organ. Satan, on the other hand, seeks to retain control of that mind which is "enmity against God." Romans 8:7.

The human mind has been compared to a computer in which the memory bank is being programmed every waking moment by one of two sources: Christ or Satan. Like the computer, the mind's function depends upon the information it receives. Having analyzed the information, the mind then determines its decision and subsequent course of action.

"Christ is the source of every right impulse."[1] In opposition, "Satan is ever seeking to impress and control the mind, and none of us are safe except as we have a constant connection with God."[2] "There are but two powers that control the minds of men—the power of God and the power of Satan."[3] "Satan takes control of every mind that is not decidedly under the control of the Spirit of God."[4]

In the clear, penetrating light of the foregoing statements, let us attempt to analyze how the two great powers of good and evil work. "Come now, and let us reason together . . ." Isaiah 1:18 is the basis of God's plan of working with the human family. "God first requires the heart, the affections."[5]

(The mind and heart are used interchangeably in Scripture as well as in the writings of Ellen White.)

"My son, give me thine heart, and let thine eyes observe my ways." Proverbs 23:26.

> "The plan of beginning outside and trying to work inward has always failed and always will fail. God's plan with you is to begin at the seat of all difficulties, the heart, and then from out of the heart will issue the principles of righteousness; the reformation will be outward as well as inward."[6] (Also see Appendix D).

Often it is said about someone who is learning how to become a Christian, "All that he has left to do is give up this or that bad habit." Possessions, attitudes or habits of life do not constitute the problem; they are only symptoms of the real problem. God says, ". . . man looketh on the outward appearance, but the Lord looketh on the heart." 1 Samuel 16:7. "Keep thy heart with all diligence; for out of it are the issues of life." Proverbs 4:23.

> "As the leaven, when mingled with the meal, works from within outward, so it is by the renewing of the heart that the grace of God works to transform the life. No mere external change is sufficient to bring us into harmony with God. There are many who try to reform by correcting this or that bad habit, and they hope in this way to become Christians, but they are beginning in the wrong place. Our first work is with the heart."[7]

We can readily see that God's method of accomplishing His goal for man is to begin with the heart or mind. Even this must be by our willing permission. "Behold, I stand at the door and knock . . ." Revelation 3:20. "If ye be willing and obedient, ye shall eat the good of the land." Isaiah 1:19. ". . . God will accept only willing service."[8]

Therefore, He cannot accept obedience that is the result of obligation, force, or even the desire to satisfy a guilty conscience.

> "The man who attempts to keep the commandments of God from a sense of obligation merely— because he is required to do so—will never enter the joy of obedience. He does not obey. When the requirements of God are accounted a burden because they cut across human inclination, we may know that the life is not a Christian life. True obedience is the outworking of a principle within. It springs from the love of righteousness, the love of the law of God."[9]

Satan's method of working began in heaven where he was successful in his effort to spread the rebellion that began in his own mind. "It was his policy to perplex with subtle arguments concerning the purposes of God. Everything that was simple he shrouded in mystery, and by artful perversion cast doubt upon the plainest statements of Jehovah."[10]

His plan worked so well that he has carried it out here on earth for nearly six thousand years.

> "The enemy is a master worker, and if God's people are not constantly led by the Spirit of God, they will be snared and taken.
>
> For thousands of years Satan has been experimenting upon the properties of the human mind, and he has learned to know it well. By his subtle workings in these last days, he is linking the human mind with his own, imbuing it with his thoughts; and he is doing this work in so deceptive a manner that those who accept his guidance know not that they are being led by him at his will. The great deceiver hopes so to confuse the minds of men and women, that none but his voice will be heard."[11]

Satan's work began in heaven by suggesting doubts, questions and thoughts in such a subtle way that the unfallen angels were not aware that they were being led by him. They uttered thoughts that originated with him, thinking they were their own.[12] Any plan that worked so well in heaven would surely work well on earth. We are witnesses to its success.

Now let us analyze these plans together. Both powers are seeking complete control of the mind to the exclusion of the other. God, by man's willing surrender to Him; Satan, by man's insistence on independence—a gift from the devil himself.

> "The enemy is preparing for his last campaign against the church. He has so concealed himself from view that many can hardly believe that he exists, much less can they be convinced of his amazing activity and power. They have to a great extent forgotten his past record; and when he makes another advance move, they will not recognize him as their enemy, that old serpent, but they will consider him a friend, one who is doing a good work. Boasting of their independence they will, under his specious, bewitching influence, obey the worst impulses of the human heart and yet believe that God is leading them. Could their eyes be opened to distinguish their captain, they would see that they are not serving God, but the enemy of all righteousness. They would see that their boasted independence is one of the heaviest fetters Satan can rivet on unbalanced minds."[13]

God says through Jesus Christ, "If the Son therefore shall make you free, ye shall be free indeed." John 8:36. Satan says, "Come on now, you don't need to be a slave to anyone."

God, by open confrontation, uses reason. Satan, by keep-ing hidden, causes man to feel that he is doing his own thinking and making his own decisions when, in fact, the opposite is the case.

In this great contest there is one thing that Satan is ex-ceedingly careful to keep hidden—his own weakness. It had been his plan to secure man's fall, and then he hoped that he and guilty man would be forgiven and be accepted back into God's favor. God had planned otherwise. Since Satan and his angels had fallen by open rebellion, and man had fallen through temptation, their guilt was not equal. Therefore, God directed that man alone would be given an opportunity to accept of the redeeming power of God's gift in His Son through the plan of salvation.

Satan soon learned that his plan had made it necessary for Jesus, God's Son, to become a human being and pay the pen-alty for sin in man's place. The devil rejoiced in this fact. However, he did have a problem. How could he now hold man in his power? Herein lies Satan's best kept secret!

At the very highest level within the mind of man God placed His most precious gift to man—the will. "This is the governing power in the nature of man, the power of deci-sion, or of choice. Everything depends on the right action of the will."[14] "Your will is the spring of all your actions."[15] With such a power in Satan's control, how easy it would be to bring man to destruction while deceiving him into think-ing he had plenty of time to change as he desired.

Now, what about the carefully kept secret? "This will, that forms so important a factor in the character of man, was at the fall given into the control of Satan; and he has ever since been working in man to will and to do of his own pleasure, but to the utter ruin and misery of man."[16]

But why is this such an important secret? Because here is the method of Satan's control without his involvement even being recognized. This is exactly the same method he used in heaven. Satan knows that God will not remove this control from him, for God will never force our will. The Lord has just one plan—to win us back to Himself. Because of His gift in giving Jesus to mankind, God can say, "Yield yourself up to Me; give me that will; take it from the control of Satan, and I will take possession of it; then I can work in you to will and to do of My good pleasure."[17]

Man must remove his will from Satan's control before he can give it to Christ. Satan well knows that he cannot retain or force man's will if man chooses to remove it from his control. "The tempter has no power to control the will or to force the soul to sin."[18] As long as Christ has control, Satan is powerless. "Satan knows that he cannot overcome man unless he can control his will."[19]

"The tempter can never compel us to do evil. He cannot control minds unless they are yielded to his control. The will must consent, faith must let go its hold upon Christ, before Satan can exercise his power upon us."[20] Here lies his weakness. "Satan is well aware that the weakest soul who abides in Christ is more than a match for the hosts of darkness, and that, should he reveal himself openly, he would be met and resisted."[21]

It must be understood that while we can remove our will from Satan, we have no power to keep it ourselves. It must be surrendered completely to Jesus. Only God alone can keep it safe from Satan's deceptions. Unless our will is decidedly in Christ, Satan will take control again. "None but Christ can fashion anew the character that has been ruined by sin. He came to expel the demons that had controlled the will."[22]

There is one more fact that we must understand clearly in regard to how Satan and his demons control the will. "Those who would not fall a prey to Satan's devices must guard well the avenues to the soul; they must avoid reading, seeing, or hearing that which will suggest impure thoughts."[23] "All should guard the senses, lest Satan gain victory over them; for these are the avenues to the soul."[24]

The five senses are the devil's playground—taste, touch, sight, hearing, and smelling—all have one common denominator—each must be reduced to feelings before it can be used of Satan to fit into his plan. He uses our feelings in place of reason to guide the will. Perhaps we should ask ourselves how many decisions we make each day through feelings rather than through the use of reason.

As we take our will from Satan's control and surrender it to Jesus, He purifies it and returns it to us linked with His own will. It is thus that He abides in us and we in Him. The result is that when doing His will, we are but doing our own.

This surrender must not be thought of as a trifling experience—something that can be done with little effort or thought. "It is through the will that sin retains its hold upon us. The surrender of the will is represented as plucking out the eye or cutting off the hand."[25]

Let us suppose that a child of God is plagued with a sinful habit that he enjoys. He knows that he should give it up and at times even prays that God will take it from him. He may even be persuaded to surrender this evil habit to God. What he needs to know is that this condition is a symptom of an unsurrendered will. He is still desiring to direct his own life and is blind to the fact that when God controls the will we still do the choosing, but it is then our greatest desire to do His will and not our own. We need to understand that our natural desire to "do our own thing" is changed to a natural desire to do His will by the surrender process. We lose nothing except a desire to please self. We gain by living on a new plane where sin has lost its power and peace reigns in the soul.

When the will is in God's control, the five senses are reduced to reason and conscience rather than feelings. We then live by faith in place of feelings. Living by faith does not do away with feelings but puts them in their proper place. They must follow the exercise of the will rather than to be the motivation for the action of the will.

Now you know the enemy's top secret! If you have never thought to take your will from Satan's control, why not do it right now? Just say audibly to Satan, "I am taking my will from your control and surrendering it to Jesus." Then say to Jesus, "Please take my will for I cannot keep it."

Jesus promises to take, purify, cleanse, and return that will to you linked with His own. "When you give up your own will, your own wisdom, and learn of Christ, you will find admittance into the kingdom of God."[26]

There is no power in heaven or earth that can force us to take this simple step. Let us keep in mind that it is the simple steps in God's plan of salvation that Satan tries to keep us from believing and implementing. His power over us can be broken with such a simple step as keeping our will surrendered to God every day. He knows that we hold the key in our hands. Will you take this step and use this key? It will open to you the power of heaven as you link yourself with God.

Notes:

1 <u>Steps to Christ</u>, p. 26.
2 <u>Testimonies</u>, vol. 4, p. 542.
3 <u>Temperance</u>, p. 276.
4 <u>Testimonies to Ministers</u>, p. 79.
5 <u>Testimonies</u>, vol. 2, p. 169.
6 <u>Counsels on Diet and Foods</u>, p. 35.
7 <u>Christ's Object Lessons</u>, p. 97.
8 <u>The SDA Bible Commentary</u>, vol. 7, p. 977.
9 <u>Christ's Object Lessons</u>, p. 97.
10 <u>Patriarchs and Prophets</u>, p. 41.
11 <u>Selected Messages</u>, book 2, pp. 352-353.
12 <u>Patriarchs and Prophets</u>, pp. 35-40.
13 <u>Testimonies</u>, vol. 5, p. 294.
14 <u>Steps to Christ</u>, p. 47.
15 <u>Messages to Young People</u>, p. 135.
16 <u>Messages to Young People</u>, p. 154.
17 <u>Messages to Young People</u>, p. 154.
18 <u>The Great Controversy</u>, p. 510.
19 <u>Temperance</u>, p. 16.
20 <u>The Desire of Ages</u>, p. 125.
21 <u>The Great Controversy</u>, p. 530.
22 <u>The Desire of Ages</u>, p. 38.
23 <u>The Acts of the Apostles</u>, p. 518.
24 <u>The Adventist Home</u>, p. 401.
25 <u>Thoughts from the Mount of Blessing</u>, p. 61.
26 <u>Selected Messages</u>, book 1, p. 110.

2.

Perfectly LEGAL

"Be ye therefore perfect even as your Father which is in heaven is perfect." Matthew 5:48. This statement from Christ's Sermon on the Mount clearly tells us that God's plan for man has never changed. He created man perfect.

When Adam fell from that state of perfection, the human family inherited his guilt. Nevertheless, man's fallen condition has not lessened one bit the perfection requirement that Jesus clearly states in Matthew 5:48.

However, God has a plan through which man can meet His requirements. That plan is simple enough to be understood by man, yet it is so comprehensive that only God can ever probe its depths. John 3:16.

Satan, by misrepresenting God's character to man, has caused that plan to be misunderstood. As a result, man has devised many methods to reach perfection. We feel sorry for the Hindu who might roll on a bed of spikes. Yet, we try to reach that same goal by doing good things that we are led to believe a good Christian should do if he expects to reach heaven.

It doesn't matter how close to the genuine a counterfeit is. A counterfeit is still a counterfeit. The closer it looks to the genuine, the more deceptive it becomes which is why "The strongest bulwark of vice in our world is not the . . . life of the abandoned sinner or the degraded outcast; it is that life which otherwise appears virtuous, honorable, and noble, but in which one sin is fostered, one vice indulged."[1]

That sin may be small. But it is not the size of the sin that is so important as is the refusal to recognize sin's malignant nature and surrender our rebellion to Jesus. It is resistance to His work in our lives that grieves His heart, for there is nothing He can do until we are willing to be yielded as the clay in the potter's hands.

God's plan is succinctly stated in <u>Steps to Christ</u>.

> "It was possible for Adam, before the fall, to form a righteous character by obedience to God's law. But he failed to do this, and because of his sin our natures are fallen and we cannot make ourselves righteous. Since we are sinful, unholy, we cannot perfectly obey the holy law. We have no righteousness of our own with which to meet the claims of the law of God. But Christ has made a way of escape for us. He lived on earth amid trials and temptations such as we have to meet. He lived a sinless life. He died for us, and now He offers to take our sins and give us His righteousness. If you give yourself to Him, and accept Him as your Saviour, then, sinful as your life may have been, for His sake you are accounted righteous. Christ's character stands in place of your character, and you are accepted of God just as if you had not sinned."[2]

Here we have God's marvelous plan in one passage. This plan, however, is more comprehensive than we see at first glance. Paul tells us, "He [God] has made known to us His hidden purpose—such was His will and pleasure determined beforehand in Christ—to be put into effect when the time was ripe: namely, that the universe, all in heaven and on earth, might be brought into a unity in Christ." Ephesians 1:10, NEB.

Think of it! The entire universe all drawn together in perfect harmony by the magnetic force of the love of God through Jesus Christ our Lord.

But this is not all. We obtain an inheritance ". . . being predestinated (pre-planned for) according to the purpose of Him [God] who worketh all things after the counsel of His [God's] own will." Ephesians 1:11. Can you imagine what is involved when we become inheritors? This means that we are actual members of His family—His flesh and bones. We are more than adopted; we are grafted into the true vine. We shall speak more of this in a later chapter.

Now since in God's plan Jesus is the cohesive power around which the entire universe revolves, and every being is bound to Him with cords of love, we can see that Christ's character of love (His robe of righteousness) given to me— a sinner, would be the only way that angels, inhabitants of other worlds and men and women of all countries of earth could agree without question that we are safe for eternity. Only as we become like Him in character can we reveal stability that cannot be shaken.

I am certain that by now we have discovered that the only way to perfection is through justification—just as if I had never sinned. I hope that it is equally clear that justification is the crediting of Christ's perfect character to an imperfect and helpless sinner.

> "What is justification by faith? It is the work of God in laying the glory of man in the dust, and do-ing for man that which is not in his power to do for himself. When men see their own nothingness, they are prepared to be clothed with the righteousness of Christ."[3]

Let us now look at the *process* of justification. The Bible says it well in one sentence. "Therefore being justified by faith, we have peace with God through our Lord Jesus Christ." Romans 5:1. In other words, Christ's death enables Him to justify everyone who wishes to be justified. "On the cross of Calvary He paid the redemption price of the race. And thus He gained the right to rescue the captives from the grasp of

the great deceiver.''[4] We can readily see that faith is only the
means and *not the basis* of justification. We do not stand on
the ground of faith, but faith enables me to stand, trusting
God's word. Faith is more real than any or all of our five
senses. (See The SDA Bible Commentary, vol 6, p. 1073.)

Now there is another side to look at when we consider
this matter of faith. Paul states, "Knowing that a man is
not justified by the works of the law, but by the faith of
Jesus Christ, even we have believed in Jesus Christ, that
we might be justified by the faith of Christ, and not by the
works of the law: for by the works of the law shall no flesh
be justified." Galatians 2:16.

Let us examine a statement from the Review & Herald,
April 24, 1888:

> "We should study the life of our Redeemer, for
> He is the only perfect example for men. We should
> contemplate the infinite sacrifice of Calvary, and
> behold the exceeding sinfulness of sin and the righ-
> teousness of the law. You will come from a con-
> centrated study of the theme of redemption strength-
> ened and ennobled. Your comprehension of the
> character of God will be deepened; and with the
> whole plan of salvation clearly defined in your mind,
> you will be better able to fulfill your divine com-
> mission. From a sense of thorough conviction, you
> can then testify to men of the immutable character
> of the law manifested by the death of Christ on the
> cross, the malignant nature of sin, and the righteous-
> ness of God in justifying the believer in Jesus on
> condition of his future obedience to the statutes of
> God's government in heaven and earth."[5]

Please read again the last sentence of the foregoing paragraph and notice upon which condition God justifies men.

We cannot understand this kind of faith. This is God's
wonderful faith in His own plan of salvation as it applies to

me—a sinner. All we can say is, "Lord, I believe, help Thou my unbelief."

I am so glad that God has given to every man *the* measure of faith. And how much faith is that? Just enough faith to reach out like the poor father with the demon- possessed son. Our faith simply opens the door for Christ to help us according to our need and His glory. Jesus is not only the author, but the finisher of our faith. Hebrews 12:2.

The process of justification is therefore a legal one. When we have a legal work to be done we must find someone qualified to do it. Jesus is the only One qualified to do our legal work. "On the cross of Calvary He paid the redemption price of the race. And thus He gained the right to rescue the captives from the grasp of the great deceiver."[6]

As the soldiers were driving the nails through the Saviour's hands, "Jesus was earning the right to become our attorney in the Father's presence."[7] Justification, being a legal work, can only deal with our legal standing (our record) and not with us personally. When a criminal is pardoned by the legal process of law, his standing before the law is changed but his character is unaffected.

For this same reason, justification is credited righteousness. This is in no way an inferior or incomplete righteousness. There is nothing that time, experience, talent or effort can add to this marvelous gift. Jesus lived in this world for thirty-three and one-half years and developed a perfect character. This is His unspeakable gift to us.

Let your imagination stretch to its utmost limits and still it is impossible to conceive of anything that you could add to that unspeakable gift of His perfection credited to us.

Here is where the human nature is tempted to believe that perfection cannot be ours in reality unless we do some of the work of developing it. There is a work, of course, a most trying and painstaking work for us to do which we will soon see clearly. However, we must keep in mind that only God can do His work and only man can do his work. It is as impossible for God to do man's work, and be consistent with His own laws, as it is for man to do God's work which he has no power to do anyway.

Sanctification—the imparted righteousness of God—is the process which clearly defines and clarifies our work from His. We will discuss sanctification in another chapter.

It is through justification that we are credited as obeying God's commandments. (See <u>Christ Our Righteousness</u>, p. 99, <u>Review & Herald</u>, August 22, 1893.)

"Therefore being justified by faith, we have peace with God through our Lord Jesus Christ." Romans 5:1. Jesus not only justifies me but also makes peace between me, the sinner, and God, my Maker whom I have been rebelling against. "The believer is not called upon to make his peace with God; he never has nor ever can do this. He is to accept Christ as his peace, for with Christ is God and peace."[8]

" . . . The carnal mind is enmity against God: for it is not subject to the law of God, neither indeed can be. So then they that are in the flesh cannot please God." Romans 8:7-8. Carnality is a term that should shock every church member into action. Contrary to common belief, carnality does not refer to the man of the world who does not know God, but rather to the man of the church who knows God but does not follow on to know Him better.

Paul refers to three levels of life of human beings: the natural man, the carnal man, and the spiritual man. 1 Corinthians 2:14, 15 & 3:1. We are all living on one of these levels. The natural is the nature we inherited from birth. The spiritual is the nature given by God when we are born again and when we continue to grow in Christ. The carnal nature is between the two. It is that new nature given to man when he is born of the Spirit and not of the flesh, but who did not grow ". . . unto the measure of the stature of the fullness of Christ." Ephesians 4:13.

This is the condition of man as described by John in Revelation 3:14-22 ". . . neither cold nor hot . . . lukewarm, and neither cold nor hot . . . I will spew thee out of my mouth . . ."

> "The figure of spewing out of His mouth means that He cannot offer up your prayers or your expressions of love to God. He cannot endorse your teaching of His word or your spiritual work in anywise. He cannot present your religious exercises with the request that grace be given you."[9]

We are well aware of the fact that unless our prayers are anointed with the Spirit of the Lord Jesus, God does not hear us. " . . . No man cometh unto the Father, but by me," said Jesus in John 14:6. This leaves us in a position where we must make a decision. This is why Jesus said, " . . . I would thou wert cold or hot." Revelation 3:15. Revelation 3:18 carefully follows with, "I counsel thee to buy of me gold tried in the fire . . ." We must keep in mind that man makes this purchase without money and without price. Isaiah 55:1.

Someone has said "victory is born out of crisis." Our crisis is to see the utter foolishness of the lukewarm condition and sense our real need of the gold God advises us to obtain. Here we need special wisdom, for many have come to this point but followed Satan's plan. They think they are walking out of their problems when he is only leading them into deeper problems.

To "turn over a new leaf," to "determine to do better," to "be more faithful" are good ideas but they are powerless to change the life.

> "As the leaven, when mingled with the meal, works from within outward, so it is by the renewing of the heart that the grace of God works to transform the life. No mere external change is sufficient to bring us into harmony with God. There are many who try to reform by correcting this or that bad habit, and they hope in this way to become Christians, but they are beginning in the wrong

place. Our first work is with the heart."[10] (See also Selected Messages, book 1, p. 353.)

The decision we must make is to allow the mind of Christ to become ours. "Let this mind be in you, which was also in Christ Jesus." Philippians 2:5.

> "God has made provision that we may become like Him, and He will accomplish this for all who do not interpose a perverse will and thus frustrate His grace."

> "With untold love our God has loved us, and our love awakens toward Him as we comprehend something of the length and breadth and depth and height of this love that passeth knowledge. By the revelation of the attractive loveliness of Christ, by the knowledge of His love expressed to us while we were yet sinners, the stubborn heart is melted and subdued, and the sinner is transformed and becomes a child of heaven. God does not employ compulsory measures; love is the agent which He uses to expel sin from the heart. By it He changes pride into humility, and enmity and unbelief into love and faith."[11]

With faith as the vehicle and love as the power, each originating with and coming from Christ, we can easily see that the process must be His also. Praise God! It is His by right of His own purchase through His willing death upon the cross. "On the cross of Calvary He paid the redemption price of the race. And thus He gained the right to rescue the captives from the grasp of the great deceiver."[12] This makes it clear that Christ took care of every conceivable legal consideration that God's holy law demanded before He attempted to rescue man from the pit of sin into which he had fallen. For Christ is " . . . the Lamb slain from the foundation of the world." Revelation 13:8.

Now, of course, we recognize that God's plan effectively

silences Satan's charges that since man had sinned, he belonged to him. Oh, the blessedness of the most precious gift God gives to man when He gives back the will that Adam surrendered at the time when he fell! This gift of a returned will enables us to choose to love, serve, and obey another master even if we know that we do not have power to accomplish that which we have chosen to do.

That choice freed God to carry out His plan to legally justify and credit to me, a sinner, His perfect character that He developed here on this earth while buffeted by the most severe temptations of Satan. That is why our record reads "just as if I'd never sinned," and Satan can do nothing about it. That is the reason why when "the Son makes you free you are free indeed."

Let me repeat: The vehicle is faith, the power is love, the process is the plan of redemption, and praise His holy name! it's legal anywhere in the entire world. It is not only legal, but it also constitutes the only source of real joy and happiness for the entire world.

Notes:

1   Thoughts From the Mount of Blessing, p. 94.
2   Steps to Christ, p. 62.
3   The Review and Herald, September 16, 1902,
       Christ Our Righteousness, p. 104.
4   Questions on Doctrine, p. 672.
5   Christ Our Righteousness, p. 35.
6   Questions on Doctrine, p. 672.
7   The Desire of Ages, p. 744.
8   Selected Messages, book 1, p. 395.
9   Testimonies, vol. 6, p. 408.
10   Christ's Object Lessons, p. 97.
11   Thoughts from the Mount of Blessing, pp. 76, 77.
12   Questions on Doctrines, p. 672

3.

HOW GOOD IS *Perfect?*

"What do ye imagine against the Lord? He will make an utter end; affliction shall not rise up the second time." Nahum 1:9. These words of Scripture constitute one of the most amazing promises found in all of the Bible.

God's Word also declares, "If the Son therefore shall make you free, ye shall be free indeed." John 8:36. This amazing promise, that man will never fail again, *will* be carried out in this freedom which He gives to us. Here we have pictured to us a time that is coming in the near future when, not even in thought, will sin raise its ugly head again.

Our first response to this thought is apt to be that with all evil removed there will be no inclination to sin, so obedience will be natural. However, this was the condition in heaven when sin started. And let me further remind you that in times of ease and prosperity man strays farthest from the Lord. Isn't this one of the major problems of the church today? "Rich and increased with goods," but destitute of love.

How is God able to make such a sweeping promise? In Malachi 4:1 God says that the cleansing fire that purifies the earth will, in the process, also remove sin—both root and branch. In John 15:5 Jesus says, "I am the vine, ye are the branches . . . ." Here Jesus was speaking to His disciples after one had separated himself from the twelve. Would it not be just as true to say that Satan is also the root from which the branches of the world are growing? These are to be consumed in the cleansing fire.

But we must look much deeper to see what is involved in God's promise of Nahum 1:9, which declares an enemy shall not arise the second time. The first enemy arose by looking to himself!

There has always been the possibility within the freedom of God's creation for the root of sin to spring up. How can God promise that not one of His redeemed, or someone from an unfallen world, or even an angel from heaven will ever, even in thought, rebel against Him? Marvel of marvels, this will be the impact of the plan of salvation throughout God's creation! God, who knows the future, assures us that this will be so.

God's work is already finished for those who dwell in the heavens. Inhabited worlds and angels have been able to rejoice that they have been liberated from the presence of evil angels and from Satan. Revelation 12:12. However, this quarantined earth and its inhabitants are fully aware of the presence of Satan and his workers.

Even so, to some of us sin has not yet become exceedingly sinful. Its deadly nature has not come through to us as malignant (deadly). Somehow we think that we can drop its bewitching influence upon us just before we are permitted to enter heaven.

"Angelic perfection failed in heaven. Human perfection failed in Eden . . . Our only hope is perfect trust in the blood of Him who can save to the uttermost all that come unto God by Him."[1] To the *uttermost* means saving *from* self not *in* self. The malignant nature of sin is revealed as we trust in self rather than in God's Word!

Could this be the reason why there is in our world today an unprecedented call from every class of society for self-expression? Nations are demanding independence. Cities, towns and villages are all declaring their own authority. Families are being broken almost as fast as they are formed.

Children are "doing their own thing" as a direct result of the self-expression atmosphere that permeates the world.

Satan is doing his work well. Thus, self-assertiveness and self-worth are declared to be the answer to personal, as well as public, problems. Think what this spirit started in heaven so long ago. "We cannot retain self and yet enter the kingdom of God. If we ever attain unto holiness, it will be through the renunciation of self and the reception of the mind of Christ."[2]

Selfish thoughts not only unfit us for heaven, but "when self is woven into our labors, then the truth we bear to others does not sanctify, refine, and ennoble our own hearts; it will not testify that we are fit vessels for the Master's use."[3]

How are we to be free from self? Hebrews 12:6 tells us, ". . . He chasteneth . . . every son whom he receiveth." This is to remove every root of bitterness (self) that could spring up to trouble us.

"See that ye refuse not him that speaketh . . ." Hebrews 12:25. How easy to hide self behind a screen of not understanding when He speaks. God does not promise that we shall understand everything before we follow His calling. Hebrews 11 reveals a large number of faithful who did not understand God's purposes, yet they all obeyed. Abel, Enoch, Noah and Abraham are just a few. Some might call this blind faith. But I would remind you that God's children ". . . walk by faith, not by sight." 2 Corinthians 5:7.

How good is perfect? Perfection is not a state of goodness to be attained, but rather a state of trusting God implicitly without doubting or questioning. It was this characteristic that marked Job's life and enabled God to say that Job was " . . . a perfect and an upright man. . ." Job 1:8.

This commendation from the Lord came in spite of the fact that Job testifies in chapter 42:6, ". . . I abhor myself, and repent in dust and ashes." Noah was declared to be ". . . just. . . and perfect . . ." Genesis 6:9. Yet, like Lot,

Moses, Abraham, David and Solomon, the Bible record of their lives reveals personal imperfection.

How good, then, is perfect? That depends.

> "As the leaven, when mingled with the meal, works from within outward, so it is by the renewing of the heart that the grace of God works to transform the life. No mere external change is sufficient to bring us into harmony with God. There are many who try to reform by correcting this or that bad habit, and they hope in this way to become Christians, but they are beginning in the wrong place. Our first work is with the heart."[4]

> "The man who attempts to keep the commandments of God from a sense of obligation merely— because he is required to do so—will never enter the joy of obedience. He does not obey. When the requirements of God are accounted a burden because they cut across human inclination, we may know that the life is not a Christian life. True obedience is the outworking of a principle within. It springs from a love of righteousness, the love of the law of God. The essence of all righteousness is loyalty to our Redeemer. This will lead us to do right because it is right—because right doing is pleasing to God."[5]

God has a plan whereby we may be found perfect—not by human effort "lest any man should boast." This perfection is a marvelous gift from Jesus Christ that is given to all who believe.

> "The law requires righteousness,—a righteous life, a perfect character; and this man has not to give. He cannot meet the claims of God's holy law. But Christ, coming to earth as man, lived a holy life, and developed a perfect character. These He offers as a free gift to all who will receive them."[6]

How good is perfect? Perfection is a divine accomplishment revealed in the life of Jesus our Lord during His earthly life on this planet. His life reveals perfect trust, total dependence upon His Father for daily living and accomplishing the will of God.

Now, He finished His work—completed everything in our behalf—knowing that we could never in our strength do what God's law requires. What is our part? Exercise the will! Choose to trust Him! Even if we know that we cannot do what we choose to do, by choosing we open the door for Christ to do in us what we are unable to do for ourselves. So, in truth, the child of God chooses to trust in all things. Then his work is to let Christ do the trusting through him and refuse to allow circumstances or situations to create doubts in the method Christ is using to do His work.

If we refuse to doubt *His methods of working* in us and simply believe He knows what He is doing, then we will have learned Christ's secret of victory—even in the face of apparent defeat.

Let me close this chapter by quoting my favorite and most helpful paragraph from the pen of one who lived what she wrote:

> "The Father's presence encircled Christ, and nothing befell Him but that which infinite love permitted for the blessing of the world. Here was His source of comfort, and it is for us. He who is imbued with the Spirit of Christ abides in Christ. The blow that is aimed at him falls upon the Saviour, who surrounds him with His presence. Whatever comes to him comes from Christ. He has no need to resist evil, for Christ is his defense. Nothing can touch him except by our Lord's permission, and 'all things' that are permitted 'work together for good to them that love God.' Romans 8:28."[7]

How good is perfect? All the goodness we will ever have is simply a perfect trust in Jesus. "Through the merits of Christ, through His righteousness, which by faith is imputed unto us, we are to attain to the perfection of Christian character."[8]

Notes:

1 The SDA Bible Commentary, vol. 5, p. 1132, The Signs of the Times, Dec. 30, 1889.
2 Thoughts from the Mount of Blessing, p. 143.
3 Selected Messages, book 1, p. 405.
4 Christ's Object Lessons, p. 97.
5 Christ's Object Lessons, pp. 97, 98.
6 The Desire of Ages, p. 762.
7 Thoughts from the Mount of Blessing, p. 71.
8 Testimonies, vol 5, p. 744.

4.

"Know ye not, that so many of us as were baptized into Jesus Christ were baptized into his death?" Romans 6:3. Most Christians who have been baptized by immersion are fully aware of being baptized in the name of the Father, Son, and Holy Spirit. But all too few are aware of the fact that baptism is into Christ's death.

Paul says, "Therefore we are buried with him by baptism into death: that like as Christ was raised up from the dead by the glory of the Father, even so we also should walk in newness of life." Romans 6:4.

Baptism symbolizes a death experience that already should have taken place in the believer's life. The death here spoken of is the death of the nature we were born with. That incorrigible old nature is fit only for death. The natural result of death is burial from which there would be no resurrection. In fact, Paul states that ". . . our old man is crucified with him, that the body of sin might be destroyed, that henceforth we should not serve sin." Romans 6:6.

> "Undoubtedly the great difficulty with the majority of believers is that they are trying to live Christ's life without first having died Christ's death. They seem to have the notion that Christ died so that we need not die, and so through faith in Christ they hope to live without dying. Paul said, 'They that are in the flesh cannot please God' Romans 8:8,

and 'they that are Christ's have crucified the flesh' Galatians 5:24."[1]

A clear understanding of the importance of this fact is absolutely necessary if we are to have a successful walk with the Lord.

> "The new birth is a rare experience in this age of the world. This is the reason why there are so many perplexities in the churches. Many, so many, who assume the name of Christ are unsanctified and unholy. They have been baptized, but they were buried alive. Self did not die, and therefore they did not rise to newness of life in Christ."[2]

The foregoing statement was written in 1897. Undoubtedly it would be equally true today. Paul states further, "Therefore if any man be in Christ, he is a new creature: (creation) old things are passed away; behold, all things are become new." 2 Corinthians 5:17.

Why is it necessary for the old nature to die? Jesus answers, "For whosoever will save his life shall lose it: and whosoever will lose his life for my sake shall find it." Matthew 16:25. Apparently there is nothing that can be done to cure the old sinful nature of man. It just simply must die. If there is to be a new life, the old must pass away.

Meade MacGuire, in his book, His Cross and Mine, gives us an insight that is very helpful.

> "There is a great difference between sins and sin. Many find serious difficulty in their Christian life because they do not understand this distinction. Beneath all our acts of transgression is the principle of sin from which they spring. Though all our evil deeds were pardoned, we would still go on sinning. Something more must be done for us than simply to pardon our sins."[3]

MacGuire continues:

> " Here it is necessary to consider the distinction between sin and sins. Sins, acts of disobedience, transgressions of the divine law, God is always ready to forgive, through the merits of Christ, in response to the prayer of penitence and faith. But sin God cannot forgive.
>
> Sin is the nature which leads us to disobey God's law. The nature with which we come into the world does not change, as we read in the Saviour's words: 'That which is born of the flesh is flesh; and that which is born of the Spirit is spirit.' The only way to be rid of a bad nature is by death. The only way to receive a good nature is to be born again."[4]

Death is the only way to deal with the old nature.

Here is how this death takes place in the believer. The lower passions have their seat in the body and work through it. The words *flesh* or *fleshly* or *carnal lusts* refer to the lower nature. We are commanded to crucify the flesh, with the affections and lusts. How? By inflicting pain on the body? No. What I want to do is to put to death the temptation to sin. Kill the corrupt thought. I want every thought controlled by Jesus Christ.[5]

In Romans 6, Paul declares that the death of the old nature is real. In verse 11 we are told to reckon this to be a fact! Here is where many Christians fail. It is so easy to believe this experience to be a theological expression, but not something that is real or practical.

Satan is responsible for this reasoning. When God states a fact, Satan will oppose, modify or attempt to change the fact to suit his cause. Satan knows that if the Christian truly believes his old nature is really dead, his power is broken.

In order to reinforce his claim that the death experience is not real, Satan tries to get the Christian to live more and more in his feelings rather than by his faith. And so he gets the believer to fall into sin. Then he turns around and blames him for falling into sin. And he uses this experience of falling as proof that the old nature is not dead. He simply uses perfectly rational reasoning and says, "If the old nature were dead, you would not have been tempted."

At this point, it is necessary for the Christian to stop trying to reason his way through the maze of feelings he has coursing through his being. He must, in spite of feelings, believe God's Word.

If he has given himself to Christ he knows that ". . . they that are Christ's have crucified the flesh with the affections and lusts." Galatians 5:24. We must always return to God's Word and stop trying to reason with Satan's suggestions if we are to remain Christians. God says that your old nature is dead even if you have fallen into sin through being tempted. Satan says that it is not dead. Now the question for us to answer is not *what* do we believe, but *who* do we believe?

How can I handle these feelings? Read chapter one again and observe the fact that Satan is the master of our feelings. The following statements underscore this fact:

> "We should daily dedicate ourselves to God and believe He accepts the sacrifice, without examining whether we have that degree of feeling that corresponds with our faith. Feeling and faith are as distinct as the east is from the west. Faith is not dependent upon feeling. We must earnestly cry to God in faith, feeling or no feeling, and then live our prayers. Our assurance and evidence is God's word, and after we have asked we must believe without doubting."[6]

In order to help us see how subtle this question of faith versus feelings is, let us think clearly as we read this next quotation:

> ". . . God must be served from principle instead
> of from feeling . . . Confound not faith and feeling
> together. They are distinct. Faith is ours to exer-
> cise. This faith we must keep in exercise. Believe,
> believe. Let your faith take hold of the blessing,
> and it is yours. Your feelings have nothing to do
> with this faith. When faith brings the blessing to
> your heart, and you rejoice in the blessing, it is no
> more faith, but feeling."[7]

The last sentence in the foregoing paragraph is not the
easiest to grasp. Please read it again. Now let's take a
closer look. Obviously, it is a very short step from faith to
feeling. Or can we say that living by faith requires constant vigilance lest we slip into living by feeling.

A clear Biblical example might help us at this point. In
Luke 10:17 the Bible says, "And the seventy returned again
with joy, saying, Lord, even the devils are subject unto us
through Thy name." Catch the excitement that must have
been shown by these returning missionaries. Never had they
had an experience like that before. Their joy must have been
very evident, for it is especially mentioned.

Now listen to Christ's response in verse 18: "And he said
unto them, I beheld Satan as lightning fall from heaven."
What a response! I can almost see the expressions on the
faces of those workers, can't you? There must have been
some talking among those men. "He must not have understood what we said. Why is He so sad? I can't figure Him
out." Some may have even tried to clarify their report.

Jesus, however, was responding from a wealth of experience that they knew nothing about. Christ's mind went back
to the fall of Lucifer and He simply was saying, "I saw that
same spirit in Satan long ago and now I am seeing it here."
To Satan had been given the blessing of great power. He
thrilled to the power but forgot the greater blessing of his
relationship to the source of that power. The key words here
that reveal the solemn truth are "subject unto us."

Listen now to verses 19 and 20: "Behold, I give unto you power to tread on serpents and scorpions, and over all the power of the enemy: and nothing shall by any means hurt you. Notwithstanding in this rejoice not, that the spirits are subject unto you; but rather rejoice, because your names are written in heaven."

The greatest blessing possible for God to bestow—a blessing that cost the life of the Son of God—was set aside and relegated to an insignificant place when compared to the casting out of devils. Calvary was the price paid that we might have our names written in heaven. The power to cast out devils Christ could give at no cost to Himself. How often we think more of a basket of groceries miraculously set on our front steps when needed, than the gift of God in allowing us to become members of His family, ". . . of his flesh, and of his bones." Ephesians 5:30.

Now that we have pointed out the problems of living by our feelings, let us return to the question of how we handle these feelings. Do we grit our teeth and bear them? Do we ignore them and hope that they will go away? Is it better to express our feelings and thereby let the tension or stress out? These and many other solutions would receive support from some very responsible people.

All our feelings are much easier to deal with by first checking their source. We must keep in mind the fact that God works first with the heart (mind) and His work is from inside outward. Satan, on the other hand, works through the feelings and his work is from the outside inward. (See Appendix D)

God motivates all of our actions through the mind. Satan motivates through the senses. He bypasses the reasoning process. Please remember, "There are but two powers that control the minds of men—the power of God and the power of Satan."[8] With these facts in mind it is easier to ascertain the source of the feelings and know what to do with them.

But how do we handle the feelings even when we know

they are from the devil? We must remember the counsel in The Adventist Home, p.128. "Put to death the temptation to sin." This is impossible for us to do in our own strength. Right here is where we must use the power of the will.

We must *choose* to believe God in spite of our feelings. Having done this, then we must frankly admit to ourselves that we cannot control our feelings. Then flee to the Lord in prayer, admitting our inability, and thank Him for His great power and willingness to deliver us. He will deliver! The feelings will pass away and peace will reign in our heart.

It may be necessary to do this often for a time until we convince Satan that we will not willingly be controlled by feelings. Walk by faith—feelings or no feelings. Keep thinking, I am dead, and my life is hid with Christ in God. Colossians 3:3. What can the devil do with a dead person? When the will is used to choose even that which we cannot do, God is glorified, for He loves to do for us that which it is not possible for us to do for ourselves.

Graveyard religion may not have much appeal for us, I'm sure it didn't for Jesus. Yet, it is the only way out of this sin problem. He said to the Greeks who came to see Him just before His death ". . . Except a corn of wheat fall into the ground and die, it abideth alone; but if it die, it bringeth forth much fruit." John 12:24.

May I suggest that your graveyard may be in your own home, workshop, office or anywhere that self may arise during each day's activities. Remaining a Christian takes much more than a daily dying to self. With Paul we must be "always bearing about in the body the dying of the Lord Jesus, that the life also of Jesus might be made manifest in our body. So then death worketh in us, but life in you." 2 Corinthians 4:10 & 12.

There is only one way to attract others to Jesus and not to ourselves. If self is hidden (crucified) Jesus is revealed. "Christ is waiting with longing desire for the manifestation of Himself in His church. When the character of Christ shall be perfectly reproduced in His people, then He will come to claim them as His own."[9]

Notes:
1 The Life of Victory, by Meade MacGuire, p. 35.
2 The SDA Bible Commentary, vol. 6, p. 1075, Manuscript 148, 1897.
3 His Cross and Mine, by Meade MacGuire, p. 80.
4 His Cross and Mine, by Meade MacGuire, p. 91.
5 The Acts of the Apostles, pp. 127,128.
6 Selected Messages, book 2, p. 243.
7 Testimonies, vol. 1, p. 167.
8 Temperance, p. 276.
9 Christ's Object Lessons, p. 69.

5.

Christians
ARE BORN NOT MADE

The born-again experience spoken of more than a dozen times in the New Testament is often grossly misunderstood. To many, it is simply believing in Jesus. To others, accepting Jesus as Saviour is to be born-again. To still others, baptism by immersion equals being born-again.

May I suggest that the new birth is such a dynamic, vitalizing experience, as pictured in God's Word, that many people find it difficult to accept literally what the Scriptures teach.

"The man who is really God's son does not practice sin, for God's nature is in him, for good, and such a heredity is incapable of sin." 1 John 3:9, Phillips.

"Everyone who believes that Jesus is the Christ is born of God, and everyone who loves the father loves his child as well." 1 John 5:1, N.I.V.

"For whatsoever is born of God overcometh the world: and this is the victory that overcometh the world, even our faith." 1 John 5:4.

We can see that being born-again is where the power of the Christian life resides. Now we must discover what makes this power a real experience to us personally. John declares, "And this is the record, that God hath given to us eternal life, and this life is in his Son. He that hath the Son hath life, and he that hath not the Son of God hath not life." 1 John 5:11, 12.

Could it be that in our eagerness to learn what is truth we have neglected to see who is the Truth? In our search for truth there may be something that is blinding us to truth. We shall try to discover what it is that blinds, so effectively, honest searchers and thus learn how to clear the way for this marvelous experience of the new birth.

"Behold, I stand at the door, and knock: if any man hear my voice, and open the door, I will come in to him, and will sup with him, and he with me." Revelation 3:20. Apparently these words are addressed to God's Laodicean church of to-day, for they are a part of the special message of Jesus to His last church. It is, therefore, imperative that we know the answer to the oft repeated question, "How am I born again?" Or is this merely a verbal experience? Is it literal? If literal, how much of my life does this give Jesus access to? My religious life? My business life? My recreational life? Just how much is necessary before He will enter my life?

> "Every thought is to be brought into captivity to Jesus Christ. All animal propensities are to be subjected to the higher powers of the soul. The love of God must reign supreme; Christ must occupy an undivided throne. Our bodies are to be regarded as His purchased possession. The members of the body are to become the instruments of righteousness."[1]

Obviously, this experience involves much more than being willing to part with our bad habits, our evil natures, our love of the world, and our earthly possessions. *Every thought* must be under His control. All natural inclinations and members of the body itself must reflect His righteousness.

In order to accomplish this, Jesus says, "I counsel thee to buy of me gold tried in the fire, that thou mayest be rich; and white raiment, that thou mayest be clothed, and that the shame of thy nakedness do not appear; and anoint thine eyes with eye-salve, that thou mayest see." Revelation 3:18.

"What is it that constitutes the wretchedness, the naked-ness, of those who feel rich and increased with goods? It is the want of the righteousness of Christ."[2] Even a strong belief in the correct doctrinal teachings of the church can-not save anyone. Jesus must have full control of every facet of our lives. This is not an arbitrary demand of our Sav-iour; it is simply one of God's divine natural laws. It is the law that says, ". . . the carnal mind is enmity against God . . ." Romans 8:7.

For this reason, Nicodemus came to Jesus by night. His heart was heavy, for he desired the covering of Christ's righ-teousness, the assurance of salvation, but he did not know how to get it. Jesus saw his need and went straight to the point. ". . . Except a man be born again, he cannot see the kingdom of God." John 3:3. Nicodemus' wealth, influ-ence, personal achievements were of no value in meeting Jesus' requirements of a new birth.

Here was Nicodemus' crisis. Unable to see the answer, he declared, " . . . How can these things be?" John 3:9. Jesus had already told him, "That which is born of the flesh is flesh; and that which is born of the Spirit is spirit." Verse 6. Nicodemus did not wish to see this. Self was very much alive in him.

Christ's statement to Nicodemus still stands. Flesh can-not crucify flesh, no matter how many promises, pledges, commitments we might make, or how much sincere ef-fort we might expend. There is always a little bit of flesh-self still alive to take over again. Someone has said that self would rather be thought evil of than not to be thought of at all.

Christ is standing at the door of His church with His voice pleading, ". . . If any man hear my voice, and open the door, I will come in . . . " Revelation 3:20. Why does Jesus pic-ture Himself thus? Because we, like Nicodemus, are still blind to self. We have yet to see that Christians are born and not made.

Many earnest Christian people have the idea that with God's help their old nature—the flesh—can be cleansed, purified, freed from the evil within and then they will be able to live victorious lives for God. This is Satan's counterfeit! His plan is to lead human beings to believe that human nature can be changed. He knows that it is only fit to die, but he tries to cover the truth with lies and keep us blinded.

"The Christian's life is not a modification or improvement of the old, but a transformation of nature. There is a death to self and sin, and a new life altogether. This change can be brought about only by the effectual working of the Holy Spirit."[3]

"Christ came to earth, taking humanity and standing as man's representative, to show in the controversy with Satan that man, as God created him, connected with the Father and the Son, could obey every divine requirement."[4]

This quotation deserves some very serious thought. In it we find the reason why it was absolutely necessary for Jesus to be born with a sinless nature such as the first Adam had. It is only that which is born of the Spirit that God can work with to mold and fashion according to His will. Sinful nature is unstable and will not respond to the Master Worker. The desire may be in the mind, but the flesh is incorrigible. The result is failure.

When Jesus said, ". . . Except a corn of wheat fall in the ground and die, it abideth alone . . ." John 12:24, He was obviously speaking of baptism which, in truth, symbolizes death.

> "The new birth is a rare experience in this age of the world. This is the reason why there are so many perplexities in the churches. Many, so many, who assume the name of Christ are unsanctified and unholy. They have been baptized, but they were buried alive. Self did not die, and therefore they did not rise to newness of life in Christ."[5] (written in 1897).

"But as many as received him, to them gave he power to become the sons of God, even to them that believe on his name: Which were born, not of blood, nor the will of the flesh, nor of the will of man, but of God." John 1:12,13. It is quite clear that Inspiration teaches the necessity of the spiritual birth before one becomes a son of God or a member of His family. However, death must precede life.

The solution to this problem is beyond man's abilities. Man, even in his sinful nature, can exercise his God-given will and choose to die and be born again.

This process is described in chapter one of this book. We had nothing to do with our natural birth but, praise God, we do have a God-given part in the born-again experience. We can choose to be born again. However, even in this new birth there must be a connection with the Father and the Son. This is what justification accomplishes.

The Father justifies the believer on the basis of his acceptance of Jesus and His atonement on the cross in the believer's behalf.

Jesus lived His life in direct connection with His Father. He said, ". . . The Son can do nothing of himself . . ." John 5:19. His life of obedience to every divine requirement was not independent from His Father but 100 percent dependent upon His Father. It is thus that His life is a perfect example for us to follow.

Jesus tells us, " . . . without me ye can do nothing." John 15:5. Independent of Jesus, even in the new birth experience, we cannot obey the divine requirements. But Jesus living in us, as the Father lived in Him, makes it possible to obey. He does this in us. And that is good news, isn't it?

The question we must ask is, "What is the divine requirement I must meet?" We find the answer in the following quotation: "God requires the entire surrender of the heart before justification can take place; and in order for man to retain justification, there must be continual obedience, through active, living faith that works by love and purifies the soul."[6]

You will notice that while the condition for justification is surrender, the condition for retaining justification is continual obedience. Does justification enable us to obey? No. Justification deals only with our legal record—our standing before God. How can we meet the second condition? Here is how:

> "As God works in the heart, and man surrenders his will to God, and cooperates with God, he works out in the life what God works in by the Holy Spirit, and there is harmony between the purpose of the heart and the practice of the life. Every sin must be renounced as the hateful thing that crucified the Lord of life and glory, and the believer must have a progressive experience by continually doing the works of Christ. It is by continual surrender of the will, by continual obedience, that the blessing of justification is retained."[7]

Please notice that man's work is to surrender his will. Christ's life was one of continual surrender. We will speak more of this in a later chapter. Continual obedience is the result of the process of sanctification, which we will consider in the next chapters. It may seem to some that human nature has been pictured as totally insignificant. That is, indeed, the point.

> "When the soul surrenders itself to Christ, *a new power takes possession of the new heart.* A change is wrought which man can never accomplish for himself. *It is a supernatural work, bringing a supernatural element into human nature.* The soul that is yielded to Christ becomes His own fortress, which He holds in a revolted world, and He intends that no authority shall be known in it but His own. A soul thus kept in possession by the heavenly agencies is impregnable to the assaults of Satan. . . . The

only defense against evil is the indwelling of Christ in the heart through faith in His righteousness. Unless we become vitally connected with God, we can never resist the unhallowed effects of self-love, self-indulgence, and temptation to sin. *We may leave off many bad habits, for the time we may part company with Satan; but without a vital connection with God, through the surrender of ourselves to Him moment by moment, we shall be overcome.*"[8]

"What is justification by faith? It is the work of God in laying the glory of man in the dust, and doing for man that which it is not in his power to do for himself. When men see their own nothingness, they are prepared to be clothed with the righteousness of Christ."[9]

"Why is it so hard to lead a self-denying, humble life? Because professed Christians are not dead to the world. It is easy living after we are dead."[10]

Remember that God's ways are not our ways. His way may look like failure, but His way is the only way to true success. For when we are truly born again—

> We live by dying.
> Strength comes through weakness.
> The battle is won by surrendering.
> Then we can know that Christians are born and not made.

Notes:

1   <u>The Adventist Home</u>, p. 128.
2   <u>Christ Our Righteousness</u>, p. 90.
3   <u>The Desire of Ages</u>, p. 172.
4   <u>The SDA Bible Commentary</u>, vol. 7A, p. 650,
    <u>The Signs of the Times</u>, June 9, 1898.
5   <u>The SDA Bible Commentary</u>, vol. 6, p. 1075,
    Manuscript 148, 1897.
6   <u>Selected Messages</u>, book 1, p. 366.
7   <u>Selected Messages</u>, book 1, p. 397.
8   <u>The Desire of Ages</u>, p. 324.
9   <u>Christ Our Righteousness</u>, p. 104.
10 <u>Messages to Young People</u>, p. 127.

6.

FROM *Justification* TO WHAT?

If one is justified and his record in heaven reads "just as if I'd never sinned," it would seem strange to desire anything added to that kind of a record. To express this kind of thinking is to reveal the fact that one is still thinking legally. There is still a desire to do something to make ourselves feel that it is real. The highest goal for the justified person is to, by faith, maintain that undeserved position that God, by His love, has given to us as a free gift. However, the moment we are justified, that moment we are also sanctified. Both of these conditions are attained solely by faith.

Justification deals with your record in heaven. It changes this record from that of a condemned criminal to that of a free man with a perfect record, including your past life.

Sanctification is heaven's ordained plan whereby the freed criminal (now a member of God's family) can continuously say thank you to God for this unspeakable gift of justification to an undeserving wretch. How does he do this? By every day allowing God to work in him according to His good will and pleasure. Philippians 2:13.

Our part is to allow God to work in our lives, rehabituating us to continuously say yes every time Jesus says, "This is the way, walk ye in it." Heaven's requirement for those who enter heaven is a complete trust in Jesus without doubting, delaying or even questioning why or how. Our response to His leading must be as natural as the flower's turning to the sun.

Obviously, there must be no doubting along the way for our justification (imputed righteousness) or our sanctification (imparted righteousness). It is through justification that obedience is credited to us, now and for the future.

> "Through His imputed righteousness, they are accepted of God as those who are manifesting to the world that they acknowledge allegiance to God, keeping all His commandments."[1]

> "We should study the life of our Redeemer, for He is the only perfect example for men. We should contemplate the infinite sacrifice of Calvary, and behold the exceeding sinfulness of sin and the righteousness of the law. You will come from a concentrated study of the theme of redemption strengthened and ennobled. Your comprehension of the character of God will be deepened; and with the whole plan of salvation clearly defined in your mind, you will be better able to fulfill your divine commission. From a sense of thorough conviction, you can then testify to men of the immutable character of the law manifested by the death of Christ on the cross, the malignant nature of sin, and the righteousness of God in justifying the believer in Jesus on condition of his future obedience to the statutes of God's government in heaven and earth."[2]

> "Personal religion among us as a people is at a low ebb. There is much form, much machinery, much tongue religion; but something deeper and more solid must be brought into our religious experience . . . What we need is to know God and the power of His love, as revealed in Christ, by an experimental knowledge . . . Through the merits of Christ, through His righteousness, which by faith is

imputed unto us, we are to attain to the perfection of Christian character."[3]

Perfection also comes through justification. It is through sanctification that this position is retained. This will be our position not only until Jesus comes but throughout eternity. It will be our happy lot to express our appreciation to the entire universe for Christ's unspeakable gift in our behalf.

Salvation is dependent upon justification as a free gift from God. Our attitude toward that gift is expressed by our relationship to sanctification and our willingness to allow Jesus to remold our characters so that they will reflect His own. This is His work no matter what methods He uses to accomplish His goal. Our work is to submit to Him.

Is sanctification the evidence of justification? Jesus, in John 15:5 says, ". . . He that abideth in me and I in him, the same bringeth forth much fruit . . ." The fruit of the Spirit is to be seen in all who are truly justified. Galatians 5:22, 23. The believer has only to abide in this relationship (position) in Christ and He will produce the fruit. Christ is the Vine; the believer is the branch. Our *position* as members of the family of God is the cause of our rejoicing. We must refuse to indulge ourselves in *conditional* thinking. When we are grafted into the Vine, we become a part of Him. Justification will always be needed. Christ's character is the only covering that could completely meet all of the demands of God's perfect law, therefore, it must always be retained.

> "The enemy of man and God is not willing that this truth [justification by faith] should be clearly presented; for he knows that if the people receive it fully, his power will be broken. If he can control minds so that doubt and unbelief and darkness shall compose the experience of those who claim to be the children of God, he can overcome them with temptation."[4]

"Behold, I give unto you power to tread on serpents and scorpions, and over all the power of the enemy . . ." Luke 10:19.

Obviously, Christians in general have not experientially been aware that they can live free from Satan's power. This does not imply freedom from his temptations. The temptations will, along with sin, have lost their *power*. This is good news for all of us.

Sin has a powerful influence in the human family. It is attractive to the sinful nature. It offers pleasure for a season. Being forbidden, it is exciting. It builds the spirit of independence. It is an abuse of the power of choice or use of the will. All these are taken care of in the truly born-again Christian as he walks with his Lord in righteousness.

There is another much more subtle aspect of the power of sin which we must consider: ". . . the strength of sin is the law." 1 Corinthians 15:56. *Dunamis* (ability) in the Greek is here translated strength. It is more often rendered power. We get our word "dynamite" from the same root. The ability of dynamite is in its explosive power. If the "strength of sin" is the law, we should know how this is true. God did not reveal His law as a transcript of His character and also the "strength of sin." God's law of love did cause Him to create man with the ability to sin. He gave him the power of choice. Could this be where the power of sin rests? "Temptation is resisted when man is powerfully influenced to do a wrong action and, knowing that he can do it, resists, by faith, with a firm hold upon divine power."[5]

It is interesting to know that the power Jesus gave His disciples recorded in Luke 10:19 was *exousia* (authority), not ability. But the power of the enemy in the same verse is *dunamis* (ability). We can say, then, that God gives men the authority over all Satan's ability, but He retains the ability and authority over Satan in His own control. Through Christ all the power of Satan is broken for he is a defeated foe.

Colossians 1:13 says, "Who hath delivered us from the power (authority) of darkness, and hath translated us into the kingdom of his dear Son." Deliverance from Satan's authority and being members of the kingdom of God are one and the same thing. "When you give up your own will, your own wisdom, and learn of Christ, you will find admittance into the kingdom of God."[6]

Since God's law is a transcript of His character, and Satan is trying constantly to misrepresent His character, we should find here a clue as to the law being the "strength of sin."

Through a misunderstanding and misuse of God's law, Israel of old was held in Satan's control for centuries of time. It was God's plan that His law, as written and revealed at Sinai, would be as a schoolmaster to bring His people to Christ. Galatians 3:24. Satan had other plans. That very law of liberty he would use to enslave. How? By focusing all of his efforts on one function of the law— its ability to convict. Paul writes, "Therefore as by the offence of one judgement came upon all men to condemnation. . ." Romans 5:18. Here is Satan's focal point and his power over men. He seeks to blind our eyes to the rest of the same verse: ". . .even so by the righteousness of one the free gift came upon all men unto justification of life."

Satan has always magnified the condemnation and then presented strict obedience to the law as the only acceptable solution to the problem. Thus, man has gone down in defeat under miserable discouragement trying to keep that which he cannot keep in his own ability—*dunamis*, or authority, *exousia*. Condemnation and guilt are associated together and form the powerhouse of Satan's work in deceiving Christians.

Conviction and guilt were intended to point man to his own nothingness, and in his extremity he would turn to God who sent His Son to solve the whole sin problem. The loving parent, when dealing with a wayward child, often reveals both authority and ability even though he be misunderstood. Sin made necessary the revealing of a law that had existed from eternity but was misunderstood and wrongly applied. By condemnation, the major function of the law as schoolmaster was hidden from human eyes.

Condemnation is a harsh, compelling force among heathen and Christian religions. Many of the reformers suffered under its power. Christianity, in general, has battled with this problem only to find human answers which fail to generate the love for God and produce a right attitude toward His law. David had his eyes opened and saw the law as the schoolmaster, or pathway, to Christ. His response was, "O how I love thy law! It is my meditation all the day." Psalm 119:97.

From the beginning of Satan's apostasy he has hated God's law, continually working to have it changed or modified. Any attempt to use justification, the imputing of Christ's character to man's account, as a means of changing or doing away with God's law is to agree with Satan and to cooperate with him in his rebellion against God.

Antinomianism, the doing away with God's law, is a human answer to man's sin problem that agrees with Satan's original accusation against God.

Modern man may think the law is incapable of meeting his needs. However, he still needs the Saviour to whom the law brings him. The truth is that man needs to be changed completely, not the law. This change is brought about in two related, but distinctly different, processes. First, a legal process was accomplished for man by Christ on Calvary's cross when He took our rightful place and paid the debt we could not pay, and yet live. Thus, man's record is changed the moment he accepts Christ as his Saviour and surrenders his life to Christ's control. "When men see their own nothingness, they are prepared to be clothed with the righteousness of Christ."[7] Calvary stands as undeniable proof of the immutability of God's law. If it had been possible to change or do away with the law, Calvary would have been unnecessary. Thank God for His gift on Calvary where Jesus gained the right to rescue the captives from the grasp of the great deceiver.[8]

"There is therefore now no condemnation to them which are in Christ Jesus, who walk not after the flesh, but after the Spirit." Romans 8:1. Justification takes care of condemnation for the surrendered Christian. The Saviour said, "For God sent not his Son into the world to condemn the world; but that the world through him might be saved." John 3:17. The law still convicts, but only Satan is in the business of condemnation. The born-again (justified) Christian learns that, even though Satan works through his feelings to condemn, Christ is not in the condemning business. "For if our heart condemn us, God is greater than our heart, and knoweth all things. Beloved, if our heart condemn us not, then have we confidence toward God." 1 John 3:20, 21.

Can we see that it is only as we understand God in His true relation to man—that of love and not condemnation— that we can have confidence in Him? This is also true of a parent-child relationship. Only in a true relationship is there true confidence. "For the law of the Spirit of life in Christ Jesus hath made me free from the law of sin and death." Romans 8:2. The law of the Spirit is to teach us about life in Christ Jesus which sets us free from the law of sin and death. This is what Paul was set free from in Romans 7.

That law of sin, which says ". . . the wages of sin is death . . ." Romans 6:23 has a terrible condemning force in our lives when pressed home by Satan. It is his plan to force us to repentance through these miserable feelings. Much of the repentance of Christians is a desire to be free from these strong feelings. If we are honest we can see that selfishness is the root of this repentance. God's Word declares, " . . . the goodness of God leadeth thee to repentance." Romans 2:4. It is not by condemnation but by looking at Jesus on Calvary's cross that we are brought to true repentance. Knowing that He condemns sin but loves the sinner sets us free. "If the Son therefore shall make you free, ye shall be free indeed." John 8:36.

As we see that we are victims of a deadly disease called sin that has left many scars called habits in our flesh—which must be eradicated—we can understand how patiently, yet persistently, Christ must work to rid us of these habits. Only then can we see why sanctification—the second process— is God's way of changing these habits of ours and is the work of a lifetime. It isn't that a lifetime would make us sinless, but it must establish in us a pattern of total surren- der and willingness which enables God to " . . . will and to do of his good pleasure" in us. Philippians 2:13.

Justification deals with our nature. As we die to self, surrender our will, and invite Him to take over our lives, a new nature is given to the newborn Christian. This nature is capable of being made subject to the law of God, whereas the old nature hated God's law. Romans 8:7. Sanctifica- tion takes over the task of rehabituating the character and removing the habits that were developed through the old nature. These habits and hereditary tendencies are the re- mainder of the old self-life. They are the strongest hold that Satan has in the life of the newborn Christian. Thank God even that hold can be broken through this marvelous plan of redemption.

Notes:

1 Christ Our Righteousness, p. 99.

2 Christ Our Righteousness, p. 35.

3 Christ Our Righteousness, pp. 81, 82.

4 Christ Our Righteousness, p. 54.

5 The SDA Bible Commentary, vol. 5, p. 1082, The Youth's Instructor, July 20, 1899.

6 Selected Messages, book 1, p. 110.

7 Christ Our Righteousness, p. 104.

8 The Desire of Ages, p. 744.

7.

LADDERS ARE FOR
Climbing

Peter's second letter is addressed to a group of people who, like himself, had obtained ". . . like precious faith with us through the righteousness of God and our Saviour Jesus Christ." 2 Peter 1:1.

It would be difficult to express in more beautiful language the fact that these people were like Peter, justified—freed from their old sins—and were walking in newness of life. Then Peter, under inspiration, clearly sets before these born-again Christians God's plan for His righteousness to be imparted to them and to us.

Peter talks plainly and authoritatively on the subject of sanctification. He makes the sweeping claim that " . . . all things that pertain unto life and godliness. . . " are given unto us. He even states fully the process by which these gifts come to the believer—by believing the great and precious promises that point us to the fact that the born-again believer can be a partaker of the divine nature.

Further, he states that he escapes the corruption of the world through this same process. 2 Peter 1:3,4. The corruption of lust spoken of here is selfishness, which is initially destroyed in the death of the old nature, by faith. This results in Jesus being able to justify the believer as he reckons himself to be dead indeed unto sin. Romans 6:12.

The believer then, according to Paul, is not only justified by the blood of Christ (His death), but he is saved by the life of Jesus. Romans 5:10. What life is that? Praise His holy name! It is His perfect life (character) that He worked out on earth for thirty-three and one-half years.

It is Jesus' character that is first credited to the believer in justification, resulting in a life record of the past that reads, "just as if I'd never sinned." This character is then made real in the believer's life as he learns to walk in this newness of life, trusting his Lord to supply the "all things" that pertain to this new life.

Of course, the goal in learning to walk in this new life is to completely rely upon the divine nature to crush out the habits of the old nature that are a carry-over from the old, but recently crucified, nature.

> "As God works in the heart, and man surrenders his will to God, and cooperates with God, he works out in the life what God works in by the Holy Spirit, and there is harmony between the purpose of the heart and the practice of the life. Every sin must be renounced as the hateful thing that crucified the Lord of life and glory, and the believer must have a progressive experience by continually doing the works of Christ. It is by continual surrender of the will, by obedience, that the blessing of justification is retained."[1]

It is quite natural, at this point, to focus upon the thought of having to be obedient. This is where the Christian often fails. Our focus should be on surrender. If we are consistent in our surrender, then God will work in us " . . . to will and to do of his good pleasure." Philippians 2:13.

Character is what we are. Reputation is what people think we are. The first is revealed by our habit patterns, the second by thoughtful control. "The character is revealed, not by occasional good deeds and occasional misdeeds, but by the tendency of the habitual words and acts."[2]

Habitual living is that which we do before we consciously think about what to do. Much of our living day by day is motivated by the subconscious mind. Our surrender to Christ's leading in our lives must become habitual. That is, it must become the natural thing to do.

"We may keep so near to God that in every unexpected trial our thoughts will turn to Him as naturally as the flower turns to the sun."[3]

Paul urges us by saying, "Let this mind be in you, which was also in Christ Jesus." Philippians 2:5. Then follows a surrender so complete that it was ". . . unto death, even the death of the cross." Verse 8.

By the word "let," we understand that the controlling power is in our hands. "Christ is waiting with longing desire for the manifestation of Himself in His church. When the character of Christ shall be perfectly reproduced in His people, then He will come to claim them as His own."[4]

This goal can only be reached through the new birth experience in the context of righteousness by faith. The credited righteousness of justification and the given righteousness of sanctification are the " . . . all things that pertain unto life and godliness . . ." 2 Peter 1:3. These marvelous gifts of God become ours as we let Him do for us that which we cannot do for ourselves.

Daniel's prayer should be ours: "O Lord, righteousness belongeth unto thee, but unto us confusion of faces. . ." Daniel 9:7. It is hard for man to face the fact that in him dwells nothing good. It is "When men see their own nothingness, they are prepared to be clothed with the righteousness of Christ."[5] When the term "two-faced" is used, we know what the speaker means. I believe that Daniel was simply saying, "Lord, no matter which face I try to wear, it all ends in confusion for it is not real."

Oh, that God would be allowed to make Himself real in us so that we could say with Paul, "For God, who commanded the light to shine out of darkness, hath shined in our hearts, to give the light of the knowledge of the glory of God in the *face of Jesus Christ.* But we have this treasure in earthen vessels, that the excellency of the power may be of God, and not of us." 2 Corinthians 4:6,7. (Italics supplied.)

Peter's ladder of sanctification is given to us in 2 Peter 1:5-7. "Add to your faith virtue; and to virtue knowledge; and to knowledge temperance; and to temperance patience; and to patience godliness; and to godliness brotherly kindness; and to brotherly kindness charity (love)." Here Peter sets before us the steps by which Bible sanctification can be attained.

> "Faith, virtue, knowledge, temperance, patience, godliness, brotherly kindness, and charity are the rounds of the ladder. We are saved by climbing round after round, mounting step after step, to the height of Christ's ideal for us. Thus He is made unto us wisdom, and righteousness, and sanctification, and redemption."[6]

Before we start ascending this ladder we must learn more of the characteristics that comprise its unique structure. Each round in this ladder is a step in character development. However, we do not perfect each stage before we move up the ladder.

We might say that this ladder is like a rope ladder hung from above. This is what makes it a ladder of faith, its support is from above. The climber beginning on the bottom rung picks up the steps one at a time as he goes, adding to his character and " . . . as he thus works on the plan of addition, God works for him on the plan of multiplication."[7]

Each step must be taken in *order* for they are tied together and are interdependent. The second depends upon the first for its foundation upon which to build. Each character step continues to be multiplied by the Lord as long as we continue to grow spiritually.

There is one thing further we need to know about this ladder:

> "Before the believer is held out the wonderful pos-
> sibility of being like Christ, obedient to all the prin-
> ciples of the law. But of himself man is utterly un-
> able to reach this condition. The holiness that God's
> word declares he must have before he can be saved,
> is the result of the working of divine grace, as he
> bows in submission to the discipline and restraining
> influences of the Spirit of truth . . . . The part of the
> Christian is to persevere in overcoming every fault.
> Constantly he is to pray to the Saviour to heal the
> disorders of his sin-sick soul. *He has not the wisdom
> or the strength to overcome; these belong to the Lord,*
> and He bestows them on those who in humiliation
> and contrition seek Him for help."[8]

Did you notice that our work is to submit to life's experiences, without complaint, accepting everything as coming from Christ even though it may have originated with
Satan? Because Christ's robe of righteousness surrounds
us, we must recognize that nothing can touch us except by
His permission. Romans 8:28.

Christ permits to touch us only that which will help our
character to become like His. (See Thoughts from the
Mount of Blessing p. 71). By accepting this truth we learn
to trust Him in every experience of life. Thus, we live by
faith and not by sight. It was thus that Jesus lived here as
our example.

Here is another picture: "This work of transformation from
unholiness to holiness is a continuous one. Day by day God
labors for man's sanctification, and man is to cooperate with
Him, putting forth persevering efforts in the cultivation of
right habits."[9] Once again God's work and man's work are
defined. God's work is the daily work of sanctification. Our
work is to cooperate by "cultivating right habits."

If we are to cultivate right habits, the natural question is, how? We might try by exercising the will, by determined effort, by repetition of the desired habit, or we might try prayer.

May I suggest that the word cultivate was, no doubt, chosen because of its depth of meaning. If we would change the wording from habits to carrots we would have less trouble understanding the how. Now if we are cultivating carrots we all know how to do that. We simply remove weeds and break up the hard soil so the carrots can grow. But what do we do with the carrots? We leave them in the Lord's care. Only He can cause them to grow. We can only remove hindrances to that growth.

> "He longs to reveal His grace. If His people will remove the obstructions, He will pour forth the waters of salvation in abundant streams through the human channels."[10]

> "There is nothing that Satan fears so much as that the people of God shall clear the way by removing every hindrance, so that the Lord can pour out His Spirit upon a languishing church and an impenitent congregation."[11]

We already have learned that we can't change ourselves. "Can the Ethiopian change his skin, or the leopard his spots? Then may ye also do good, that are accustomed to do evil." Jeremiah 13:23. Our work in removing hindrances and obstacles in our character formation is to recognize them when we see them. Then we are to be persevering in our prayers to God to heal our sin-sick souls. He will remove these hindrances when we are ready to stop protecting these hindering factors. We need to recognize a weed from the true plant.

The fruits of the Spirit are tender plants that need careful cultivation until they are well rooted. Then they become dominant to the point where we can say with Paul, " . . . none of these things move me . . ." Acts 20:24.

All this preparatory work, as well as the climbing of Peter's ladder, is a work of faith. "There are those who attempt to ascend the ladder of Christian progress; but as they advance, they begin to put their trust in the power of man, and soon lose sight of Jesus, the author and finisher of their faith. The result is failure." (See <u>The Acts of the Apostles</u>, p. 532.)

Let us clearly understand that sanctification, like justification, is a work of faith at every step.

> "The followers of Christ are to become like him— by the grace of God to form characters in harmony with the principles of His holy law. This is Bible sanctification. This work can be accomplished only through faith in Christ, by the power of the indwelling Spirit of God."[12]

> "In ourselves we are incapable of doing any good thing; but that which we cannot do will be wrought by the power of God in every submissive and believing soul. It is through faith that spiritual life is begotten, and we are enabled to do the works of righteousness."[13]

> "None but Christ can fashion anew the character that has been ruined by sin. He came to expel the demons that had controlled the will."[14]

> "It is through the impartation of the grace of Christ that sin is discerned in its hateful nature, and finally driven from the soul temple."[15]

These statements make it very clear that only as Christ's character is imparted to us in sanctification are we able to see sin for what it really is—a malignant disease. Only then can we learn to hate it. This fact will become clear as we begin to ascend the ladder.

You will notice sin is in the singular, which points to the disease and not sins, which are the symptoms of the disease. We can very easily work up quite a strong feeling of hatred for the sins that reveal that there is a sinful nature from which they spring. Yet our efforts are most often directed toward the symptoms and not the disease. And this is what Satan would have us do. For until the disease is taken care of, he knows that the symptoms will be there to keep us battling and defeated.

It is a fact that we overlook the reality that every human being in his human (fleshly) nature is infected with the same deadly disease of sin. From God's viewpoint the disease in any stage is still deadly. Some symptoms, however, are quite acceptable in the best of society, while others would be rejected as making one incorrigible.

God must be allowed to reveal to us this deadly nature and bring us to the point where we look at sin as He does. Then we will long to be free from its vicious tentacles. Why is this so hard for human beings to see? Because we are sin-hardened, calloused to the point where we hardly recognize sin when we come in contact with it. The tragedy of this is the fact that as we live in this condition we forget that "He [Christ] was free from the taint of sin, the refined sensibilities of His holy nature rendered contact with evil unspeakably painful to Him."[16] What a work must be accomplished in us that we might reflect His image perfectly.

Before we begin climbing this ladder of sanctification, let us take an overview of the chart (Appendix C, pages 154, 155). Here we attempt to show how Satan has a counterfeit plan for sanctification as he does for every Bible truth. God's plan begins with faith and ends with love (divine love). Satan's plan begins with self, very much alive, and ends with emotionalism.

Satan's plan develops hindrances, obstacles, that prevent the Christian from developing the character of Christ. These characteristics become stronger and stronger, thus preventing the end result of divine love from being attained. In its place is a very entrancing, bewitching, and deceptive substitute which we call emotionalism. It is in this area of emotional living where Satan holds spellbound millions of deceived Christian people.

I do not mean to convey the thought that there is no emotion in the way of the Lord. There truly is. But it is the love of Christ that constraineth us. 2 Corinthians 5:14. That is, the love of Christ holds us together. This is the effect of divine love.

Emotionalism tends toward strong feelings, especially toward those who understand each other. The love of Christ, on the other hand, reaches out and engulfs even those who oppose and even fight against us. It accepts any kind of treatment and still reacts only with love. Obviously, this is not natural to the human being. It must be a gift from God. That is what sanctification accomplishes.

We must remember also that the Christian, while allowing God to develop His character in man, grows *in grace* (God's character), *not into grace* (God's character)[17] The growth process is hard to recognize as it operates, but the result is evident both to the believer and to those with whom he comes in contact.

Keep in mind as we ascend the ladder that each step is one of faith as is shown in the statements between the two ladders on our chart.

Yes, ladders are for climbing, and we are about ready to begin. So let us pray that God will reveal any hindrances or obstacles that would prevent His working in us to produce the fruit of righteousness. It might be a good idea to take a quick look at the character fruit we can expect to be revealed as He does this marvelous work in us. ". . . The fruit of the Spirit is love, joy, peace, longsuffering, gentleness, goodness, faith, meekness, temperance . . . ." Galatians

5:22,23.

Notes:

1   Selected Messages, book 1, p.397.

2   Steps to Christ, pp. 57, 58.

3   Steps to Christ, pp. 99, 100. (Italics supplied.)

4   Christ's Object Lessons, p. 69.

5   Christ Our Righteousness, p. 104, The Review and Herald, September 16, 1902.

6   The Acts of the Apostles, p. 530.

7   The Acts of the Apostles, p. 532.

8   The Acts of the Apostles, p. 532. (Italics supplied.)

9   The Acts of the Apostles, p. 532.

10 The Desire of Ages, p. 251. (Italics supplied.)

11 Selected Messages, book 1, p. 124.

12 The Great Controversy, p. 469.

13 The Desire of Ages, p. 98.

14 The Desire of Ages, p. 38.

15 Selected Messages, book 1, p. 366.

16 The SDA Bible Commentary, vol. 7A, p. 451, The Review and Herald, Nov. 8, 1887.

17 Christ's Object Lessons, p. 271.

8.

A SOLID FOUNDATION
"Add to Your Faith"

Before climbing a ladder, one needs to examine the foundation upon which it rests! Since the first step of the ladder is faith, let us begin with the premise that the foundation itself is faith.

Peter is addressing his message to those who, like himself, have been justified by faith. But we hear someone say, "You already told us that this ladder hangs from above and is not supported from beneath." This is true. That is why the foundation is faith. Paul said ". . . the life which I now live in the flesh I live by the faith of the Son of God . . . " Galatians 2:20. We must keep in mind that the foundation, as well as every step in this ladder, is by the faith that is from above. In fact, " . . . in him we live, and move, and have our being . . . " Acts 17:28. " . . . Ye are not your own, for ye are bought with a price . . . " 1 Corinthians 6:19-20. That price is the blood shed at Calvary, that Christ might be legally qualified to justify us and deliver us from ourselves. The thought that we need to be delivered from ourselves may be hard for some of us to accept.

God's picture of ancient Israel reveals our condition today: ". . . The whole head is sick, and the whole heart faint. From the sole of the foot even unto the head there is no soundness in it; but wounds, and bruises, and putrefying sores: they have not been closed, neither bound up, neither mollified with ointment." Isaiah 1:5-6.

Are we not thankful that in God's plan of justification

the old man really dies? We are then given a new life in Christ as Paul states, "Therefore if any man be in Christ, he is a new creature: (creation) old things are passed away; behold, all things are become new." 2 Corinthians 5:17. This is a fact based on the promise of God. This, according to Peter, enables us to become partakers of the divine nature.

We must constantly keep in mind that we are new persons in Christ. In the climbing of Peter's ladder, over and over again, we will be conscious of a strong power working in our members that will war against the Spirit's leading in this walk of faith. We may often cry out as Paul did, "O wretched man that I am! Who shall deliver me from the body of this death?" Romans 7:24.

It is essential for us to remember that the battle between Christ—the new ruler of the new man—and Satan—the deposed ruler of the old man—is still raging with even increased activity, for *Satan is angry*. His old method of control in our lives was through our habit patterns. We must never forget that character is revealed in our habits.

> "The temper, the personal peculiarities, the habits from which character is developed—everything practiced in the home will reveal itself in all the associations of life. The inclinations followed will work out in thoughts, in words, in acts of the same character."[1]

Again we read:

> "The defects cherished in dealing with life's minor details pass into more important affairs . . . . Thus actions repeated form habits, habits form character, and by the character our destiny for time and for eternity is decided."[2]

With these facts firmly in mind, we can clearly see that the battle is over who is controlling the mind. We then must have a clear mind in order to discern the difference between the two powers striving for the supremacy. Now, let us be perfectly honest with ourselves and analyze to determine if most of our decisions in life have been made on the basis of principle or on feelings. If we are honest, we find that feelings have often had a great deal to do with even spiritual decisions. These feelings, that have been the avenue through which Satan has held control, have formed strong habit patterns and Satan will not let these die without a real battle. Our response to any given situation will first be triggered by our accustomed habitual life. If we act in harmony with our feelings, Satan takes advantage of the situation that he has created and then uses our habit response to accuse, condemn and discourage us. He thus tries to make us believe that our justification is not genuine and that we must be fooling ourselves.

The born-again Christian, living by faith, must school himself to do what angels counseled Adam and Eve to do when Satan would tempt them. This is where our battle seems almost overwhelming. Our first parents failed, however, in Christ, we may succeed! How? Adam and Eve were told to repel Satan's first insinuations, then they would be secure.[3] We must recognize the enemy at work in the habitual responses and, knowing our weakness, turn immediately to Christ for help. We must admit that we cannot win by resistance, no matter how we try to control our feelings! When we face our weakness and turn the situation over to Christ, He uses the same situation instantly as a tool in His hand to form our character. "None but Christ can fashion anew the character that has been ruined by sin. He came to expel the demons that had controlled the will."[4]

In the whole climbing process Christ is at work forming this new character while we are kept busy surrendering to His working process. This is a full time responsibility for each of us. It is only as we, through surrender, open the door that He can do His work in His own new creation. We must be constantly willing to remove the obstacles and hindrances that prevent His working in our lives. Even in the surrender there is a real sense of satisfaction in knowing that "the God of peace, that brought again from the dead our Lord Jesus, that great shepherd of the sheep, through the blood of the everlasting covenant, make you perfect in every good work to do his will, working in you that which is well pleasing in his sight, through Jesus Christ; to whom be glory for ever and ever. Amen." Hebrews 13:20-21.

Even as Jesus was victorious through surrender, when to all human eyes it seemed a defeat and failure, so we have only one road to victory. This ladder is going to be tough climbing, not because it is steep and rough or rugged, but because self will keep trying to do God's work instead of doing its own—that of surrender.

There are hindrances that must be removed before one can begin the ascent of this ladder. If self is not dead through justification, we will not be able to climb Peter's ladder but will find ourselves starting up the wrong ladder.

> "The new birth is a rare experience in this age of the world. This is the reason why there are so many perplexities in the churches. Many, so many, who assume the name of Christ are unsanctified and unholy. They have been baptized, but they were buried alive. Self did not die, and therefore they did not rise to newness of life in Christ."[5]

Paul states, "If we have been planted together in the likeness of His death, we shall be also in the likeness of His resurrection." Romans 6:5. He further states, ". . . We were reconciled to God by the death of His Son, much more, being reconciled, we shall be saved by His life." Romans 5:10. While justification takes care of all the legal work, sanctification—the impartation of the life of Christ—is the process by which our fitness for heaven is determined. Justification without sanctification has no continuing saving value, and sanctification without justification is impossible.

"God requires the entire surrender of the heart, before justification can take place; and in order for *man to retain justification*, there must be continual obedience, through active, living faith that works by love and purifies the soul."[6] This is the process of sanctification.

> "Here the truth is laid out in plain lines. This mercy and goodness is wholly undeserved. The grace of Christ is freely to justify the sinner without merit or claim on his part. Justification is a full, complete pardon of sin. The moment a sinner accepts Christ by faith, that moment he is pardoned. The righteousness of Christ is imputed to him, and he is no more to doubt God's forgiving grace."[7]

If you have not experienced justification by faith, the complete unconditional surrender of yourself to Christ and accepted His death at Calvary as your death to self, let me suggest that you bow your head right now and enter into His victory planned for you.

Notes:
1 Testimonies, vol. 6, p. 174.
2 Christ's Object Lessons, p. 356.
3 See Patriarchs and Prophets, p. 53.
4 The Desire of Ages, p. 38.
5 The SDA Bible Commentary, vol. 6, p. 1075, Manuscript 148, 1897.
6 Selected Messages, book 1, p. 366. (Italics supplied.)
7 The SDA Bible Commentary, vol. 6, p. 1071, The Signs of the Times, May 19, 1898.

9.

LET'S BROADEN THE FOUNDATION
"*Virtue*"

When the Christian comes to Christ in full surrender, he accepts Christ as his Saviour from sin. His concern is primarily eternity. In Christ he now feels secure and no longer needs to worry about "making it" to heaven. Relief is blessed and reassuring. This may last for only a short time or it may be permanent. However, there will come to the earnest seeker for truth, the fact that the Christian's life is not in a "rocking chair" but in the rugged, every day life in this world of sin. He soon learns that it is one thing to be a Christian in the company of Christians—friends who are pulling for him, praying for him, and trying to encourage him. He later learns that it is another thing to live the life in different circumstances. He even finds that his own home is not as easy a place to live the Christian life as in the church or Bible study group where he learned of Christ. He may find that his job requires decisions that are embarrassing to him now that he belongs to Christ. Opportunities come to him whereby he could benefit himself greatly with only a very small compromise in his new way of life. The natural thing to do in each case would be to turn to reason. It is so difficult for us to remember that faith is not human reasoning. It requires divine reasoning to find the right answers. Jesus said, "Come now, and let us reason together . . . " Isaiah 1:18. "You have trusted Me for your salvation. Will you trust Me to take care of your daily needs as well? Will you let Me have control of every facet of your life?" He promises that if we will do this He will supply all of our needs, plus an abundant entrance into the kingdom of heaven.

This, of course, does not mean that the "rocking chair" is the answer after all. It is a comforting thing to know, however, that I am to yield myself as fully to Christ now, in the new life of faith, as I yielded myself to iniquity before I came to Jesus. Paul says, " . . . For as ye have yielded your members servants to uncleanness and to iniquity unto iniquity; even so now yield your members servants to righteousness unto holiness." Romans 6:19.

Jesus lived that completely yielded life, yet He was ambitious, energetic, careful to do the best work that He could do. He was never content with mediocrity. So, the born-again Christian will do his best, even if he sees no advantage to himself. His reward is of a higher nature than the world values. God can, and will, place such a person in positions of responsibility where His own glory (character) as seen through the human instrument will be a magnetic influence to draw men and women to Christ.

We have stated before that Christ works from the inside outward. (See Apendix D) He is following this plan in sanctification as outlined in Peter's ladder. The first three steps have to do with mental attitudes. If the mind is yielded to Him there will be no problem with the flesh. "Let this mind be in you, which was also in Christ Jesus." Philippians 2:5. Notice that this is a "letting"—a surrender of our own habitual thinking patterns. The new life of faith reaches into every corner of life's experiences. It trusts Christ even if we do not understand how He can or will do His work. Real faith is never concerned with the methods which He uses—only the results which He promises.

There are hindering factors to this kind of faith. Doubt is one of Satan's most successful tools. Have you noticed that when Satan works with a non-believer he tries to turn him away entirely from Christ, the Bible and truth? However, when he works with a Christian, he works through creating doubt. He worked this plan with Eve. He was, at first, careful not to contradict God. He simply said enough to cast doubt as to why God had said what He said. After creating the doubt in Eve's mind there came the denial of truth. She had been warned to resist the first insinuation of the enemy. She felt the impulse to flee to her husband—Adam. She then felt that if she should meet the enemy she had sufficient strength to withstand him. Now, facing him in the disguised form, she found herself arguing with him.[1] There is nothing Satan delights to do more than to entice the Christian to enter into controversy with him. "He tempts men to distrust God's love and to doubt his wisdom. He is constantly seeking to excite a spirit of irreverent curiosity, a restless, inquisitive desire to penetrate the secrets of divine wisdom and power."[2]

> "There is but one course for those to pursue who honestly desire to be free from doubts. Instead of questioning and caviling concerning that which they do not understand, let them give heed to the light which already shines upon them, and they will receive greater light."[3]

Our responsibility is to walk by faith, which requires obedience, even if we do not understand the "why."

Hebrews 11, the great faith chapter, declares that faith "is" not "has" substance and evidence. It may be hard for us to see these two characteristics of faith. Our tendency is to try to check up to see if we really have faith. Where do we check? Most of the time we check our feelings! We say, "I feel this way or that way." Our faith must rest upon something much more reliable than feelings. These constitute the devil's playground. "Faith includes not only belief but trust."[4] "The devils also believe, and tremble." James 2:19. Their belief is obviously not faith.

Why is this understanding so important to Peter's ladder? Because, "None but Christ can fashion anew the character that has been ruined by sin."[5] The real question that must be answered by each of us is, are we willing for Him to do His work in us, or will we insist on doing part of the work ourselves? The inclination will be to "get in there and help." But we must be willing to let the Potter have His way entirely and be happy to lie dormant in His hands. Then, and only then, will the product formed be of any value!

Notes:

1 See <u>Patriarchs and Prophets</u>, pp. 53-55.
2 <u>Patriarchs and Prophets</u>, pp. 54, 55.
3 <u>The Great Controversy</u>, p. 528.
4 <u>Selected Messages</u>, book 1, p. 389.
5 <u>Desire of Ages</u>, p. 38.

10.

POWER SUPPLY UNLIMITED

"Knowledge"

Jesus prayed, " . . . this is life eternal, that they might know thee the only true God, and Jesus Christ, whom thou has sent." John 17:3. John again testified, "Beloved, let us love one another: for love is of God . . . for God is love." 1 John 4:7,8. Every born-again Christian, of necessity, has come to realize that if he is to reflect the character of God, love must be naturally reflected in every facet of his life. This love is not a pretense—something put on—it must come from the inside and its source can only be Christ. The Christian cannot develop this love; it is a gift from God that comes by knowing Him.

> "The knowledge of God as revealed in Christ is the knowledge that all who are saved must have. It is the knowledge that works transformation of character. This knowledge, received, will re-create the soul in the image of God. It will impart to the whole being a spiritual power that is divine . . . "[1]

Such knowledge grows in relationship where faith is the active ingredient that binds the parties closer together with each new experience. Did you notice that it is the knowledge of God, as revealed in Christ, that we must have and that will reproduce the divine character in man? Could it be that this is the reason that we are admonished to spend a thoughtful hour each day reading and meditating upon the life of Christ, especially the closing scenes?

Such an experience would reveal to us the fact that Jesus, as a human being, learned about God first from His mother, then, as he grew older, from nature. As He learned to read, He learned about God from the Scriptures. His Father enlightened His study and revealed to Him His mission on earth. This knowledge did not, in the least, detract from His faithfulness in helping to carry His part of the family burdens. He became efficient as a tradesman and labored to help support the family until He began His public ministry.

We will discover that the more He learned of God, the more submissive He became until, finally, in the garden of Gethsemane His submission was complete when He cried, "Father, if thou be willing, remove this cup from me; nevertheless not my will, but thine, be done." Luke 22:42.

> "We should study the life of our Redeemer, for He is the only perfect example for men. We should contemplate the infinite sacrifice of Calvary, and behold the exceeding sinfulness of sin and the righteousness of the law. You will come from a concentrated study of the theme of redemption strengthened and ennobled. Your comprehension of the character of God will be deepened; and with the whole plan of salvation clearly defined in your mind, you will be better able to fulfill your divine commission. From a sense of thorough conviction, you can then testify to men of the immutable character of the law manifested by the death of Christ on the cross, the malignant nature of sin, and the righteousness of God in justifying the believer in Jesus on condition of his future obedience to the statutes of God's government in heaven and earth."[2]

A careful reading of the aforementioned quotation will reveal four things that we should especially study in relation to the life of Christ: (1) His infinite sacrifice, (2) the sinfulness of sin, (3) the righteousness of the law, (4) the theme of redemption. If we make this knowledge the target of our study, we are promised four specific returns: (1) We will be strengthened and ennobled, (2) a deepened comprehension of God's character will be ours, (3) the plan of salvation will be clearly defined, (4) we will be better able to fulfill our divine commission. Then we will be able, because of a personal conviction, to testify to the three great principle of God's plan of salvation: (1) the immutable character of God's law, (2) the malignant nature of sin, (3) God's plan of righteousness by faith. These principles reveal to us the justice and mercy of God's character which He desires to reproduce in every believer.

God has provided every incentive that He can to encourage us to enter into this study plan. Romans 5:1,2 assures the justified believer of peace with God and also the privilege of standing in God's (imputed) character during the process of sanctification. Romans 8:1,2 assures the Christian who is in the process of sanctification (walking with Jesus) freedom from condemnation and the greatest blessing possible—the Spirit to teach him how to walk with Jesus. For the very law of the Spirit is "life in Christ Jesus."

It was Jesus, Himself, who said, "But the Comforter, which is the Holy Ghost, whom the Father will send in My name, He shall teach you all things, and bring all things to your remembrance, whatsoever I have said unto you." John 14:26. It is the work of the Holy Spirit to reveal to us what "life in Christ Jesus" is all about.

The knowledge of God as revealed in Christ Jesus is the clearest, most understandable and most available to man of all knowledge. It is written on every flower, every tree, the starry heavens, the sunlight, the ocean depths and upon every creature that comes from the hand of God. It is written in His own book—the Holy Bible. Also, God has sent the third member of the Godhead to be our Instructor whether we are reading from His book of nature or the written Word. His one goal is to help us to see what "life in Christ" truly is.

Right now, as you are reading these lines, you may be having feelings that your mind can be interpreting in such a way as to cause you to procrastinate in seeking for this knowledge. These feelings constitute the greatest hindrance to our reaching the goal.

We feel that we do not have time. We feel that we cannot understand. We feel that we are alone—if only there were someone to study with. We may feel that if our life is greatly changed, we will be ridiculed or rejected. These are all feelings sent by Satan, for he knows well the power of feelings. May I remind you that feelings and faith are contrary to each other, as far apart as the east is from the west. So, in spite of feelings, seek the knowledge which is from above and be set free to experience "life in Christ Jesus" which is love unlimited—the true power of God.

When we walk with Jesus, we must remember that He does not condemn us even if we make a mistake. He is our heavenly Parent who stands ready to help us, by turning our mistakes into stepping stones instead of stumbling blocks.

Satan is the great accuser. God's Word says, "For God sent not his Son into the world to condemn the world; but that the world through him might be saved." John 3:17.

Just knowing Him has turned savages into loving, lovable Christians. No other knowledge on earth or in heaven can do this. Oh! how we need to know Him whom to know is life eternal.

Notes:
1 My Life Today, p. 293.
2 Christ Our Righteousness, p. 35.

11.

FIRST THINGS FIRST
"Temperance"

The knowledge of God as learned through the study of Christ's life leads us naturally to invite Christ to reproduce His character in us. As Christ, through faith, has been transforming the mind—bringing it into harmony with His own mind—so now, He begins to change our very life-style. This work must begin with man's greatest need.

"Temperance alone is the foundation of all the graces that come from God, the foundation of all victories to be gained."[1]

A clear definition of temperance is essential at this point.

> "True temperance teaches us to dispense entirely with everything hurtful, and to use judiciously that which is healthful. There are few who realize as they should how much their *habits* of diet have to do with their health, their character, their usefulness in this world, and their *eternal destiny*. The appetite should ever be in subjection to the moral and intellectual powers. The body should be servant to the mind, and not the mind to the body."[2]

"Intemperance . . . includes the hurtful indulgence of any appetite or passion."[3]

It is necessary to keep clearly in mind the fact that the battle between Christ and Satan is over who will control the mind of man. It would be natural, then, for Satan to do everything he could do to injure or weaken the ability of man's mind. If he can cause the mind to function at a level below its God-given capacity, he has then gained a tremendous advantage over God. If the mind cannot understand the things of God, how can it arrive at a valid conclusion? It follows that the will could not be used in a constructive way. Satan knows that if the will is not used in a positive way, he has the advantage. By creating doubts, peer pressures, etc., he can cause us to put off a decision. He is careful not to let us know that putting off a decision is really making a decision. It is exercising the will, but to his advantage.

> "You should use the most simple food, prepared in the most simple manner, that the fine nerves of the brain be not weakened, benumbed, or paralyzed, making it impossible for you to discern sacred things, and to value the atonement, the cleansing blood of Christ, as of priceless worth."[4]

"Intemperance commences at our tables in the use of unhealthful food."[5] Temperance, then, must strike at the root of the problem and from there spread to the entire lifestyle.

A perfectly balanced eight-point program was sent to us from God nearly seventy-five years ago to keep our mental and physical health functioning at top level. "Pure air, sunlight, abstemiousness, rest, exercise, proper diet, the use of water, trust in divine power—these are the true remedies."[6]

An almost unlimited amount of inspired information on this plan is open for our study in the Bible and the writings of Ellen White. If we accept these sources as authoritative, we then have a guide by which to measure all other information.

Modern research has finally validated God's health plan, and abundant material is available regarding each part of the plan. God has enlightened men and women who have written authoritatively, yet in understandable language, on the different facets of this plan. We are today without excuse.

However, we shall confine ourselves to man's greatest weakness—his appetite. If this is brought under the control of Christ, we will be victorious over every defiling sin.

> "The controlling power of appetite will prove the ruin of thousands, when, if they had conquered on this point, they would have moral power to gain victory over every other temptation of Satan."[7]

Webster defines temperance as "habitual moderation in the indulgence of appetites or passions." He defines appetite as "an inherent craving." It is as we see this close relationship, and the broad platform that appetite covers, that we can understand the above quotation.

Eve was tempted upon appetite. However, the real appetite was, no doubt, revealed in her unspoken question. Why had God withheld the fruit of this tree from them? It was this unspoken question, revealed in her attitude and expression, that prompted Satan to take advantage of the situation. "Yea, hath God said, Ye shall not eat of every tree of the garden?" Eve was captivated as she heard the serpent vocalize her own thoughts. How many today have an appetite to know the "why" of God's ways. "The secret things belong unto the Lord our God: but those things that are revealed belong unto us and to our children forever . . . " Deuteronomy 29:29. When will we be content to believe what God says and leave the "why" until He chooses to reveal it to us?

Eve's appetite revealed itself in other ways too. The serpent continued in a pleasing voice to praise her loveliness, *which she enjoyed.*

When appetite was partially fed, it was only a step to creating doubt in Eve's mind, for she was conditioned to believe the voice that revealed such *"good" judgement.* She now answered the serpent's subtle question, " . . . We may eat of the fruit of the trees of the garden; but of the fruit of the tree which is in the midst of the garden, God hath said, Ye shall not eat of it, neither shall ye touch it, lest ye die." Genesis 3:2,3. The serpent's reply was quick and forceful, " . . . Ye shall not surely die." Genesis 3:4. This direct contradiction to God's statement was then reinforced by the implantation of a doubt, "For God doth know that in the day ye eat thereof, then your eyes shall be opened, and ye shall be as gods, knowing good and evil." Genesis 3:5.

> "He [Satan] is constantly seeking to excite a spirit of irreverent curiosity, a restless, inquisitive desire to penetrate the secrets of divine wisdom and power. In their efforts to search out what God has been pleased to withhold, multitudes overlook the truths which he has revealed, and which are essential to salvation."[8]

The doubt had found lodging in Eve's mind. But Satan must reinforce the doubt with feelings. Take another look at the ladder Satan tries to get us to climb.

He now took advantage of Eve's own argument and plucking the fruit, the serpent put it in the hand of Eve. (Notice how feelings destroy knowledge.) The serpent reminded Eve of her own words, "ye shall not touch it lest ye die." Satan speaking: "There it is in your hands and you haven't died. Eating is no different." She could detect no harm from what she had done so she grew bolder. Her mind remembered the serpent's statement that the fruit would make one wise so she ate. Now come the feelings. (Please keep in mind that the feelings are Satan's special avenue through which he works.) Eve felt no evidence of God's displeasure; she experienced an exhilaration which ran through her whole body. She even imagined that this was the way heavenly beings felt.

Have you ever felt the exhilaration of an indulged moment of sin? Satan has lost none of his power.

Eve, under the spell of feelings, became the instrument through which Adam fell. Through feelings Satan is still destroying or modifying the knowledge of God as revealed to man. "Whether therefore ye eat, or drink, or whatsoever ye do, do all to the glory of God." 1 Corinthians 10:31.

Temperance would naturally follow knowledge in our lives if we would be willing to face the appetite problem. Of ourselves, we are helpless, but we have One by our side who is mighty to save. If we face our helplessness, and by an act of the will choose to apply the above Scripture, even if we have failed ever so many times, God will bring our appetites under His control. Victory will then be ours. We will have dealt with "first things first."

Notes:
1 <u>Temperance</u>, p. 201.
2 <u>Temperance</u>, p. 138. (Italics supplied.)
3 <u>Temperance</u>, p. 137.
4 <u>Testimonies</u>, vol. 2, p. 46. See also <u>Counsels on Diet and Foods</u>, p. 55 and <u>Testimonies</u>, vol. 6, p. 327.
5 <u>Testimonies</u>, vol. 3, p. 487.
6 <u>The Ministry of Healing</u>, p. 127.
7 <u>Temperance</u>, p. 16.
8 <u>Patriarchs and Prophets</u>, pp. 54, 55.

12.

Patience
– GOD'S PERFECT WORK

At this point in the climbing process—sanctification—it is essential to remember that this is a total work of faith. It is only as we do our part—recognizing the obstructions and hindering factors, then realizing that we cannot remove them ourselves—that we exercise the power of the will and choose to be free from these encumbrances. Only then can God do His work in us. He will never force the will but waits for us to use it to permit Him to remove these. We have just discovered that if this work is done at all, He will have to do it. Remember, we have "not the wisdom or the strength to overcome" evil.[1] This must be kept clearly in mind as we face each step.

Peter says, "Add . . . to temperance patience . . ." 2 Peter 1:16. "The most precious fruit of sanctification is the grace of meekness."[2] A quick look in <u>Webster's Collegiate Dictionary</u> will convince anyone of the close relationship of patience and meekness.

Without doubt, God was able to develop this trait of His character in Moses more perfectly than in any other human being. However, even in him one failure, even though he was forgiven, prevented God from being able to fulfill His plans for Moses' life here on this earth. We see here a perfect blend of God's justice and mercy. "Genuine sanctification . . . is nothing less than a daily dying to self and daily conformity to the will of God."[3]

This principle of sanctification strikes right at the very root of the problem of this step of patience, for the greatest hindering factor is pride. We have heard of impetuous Peter—the man who always spoke and acted before he thought.

> "The evil that led to Peter's fall and that shut out the Pharisee from communion with God is proving the ruin of thousands today. There is nothing so offensive to God or so dangerous to the human soul as pride and self-sufficiency. Of all sins it is the most hopeless, and the most incurable."[4]

Pride and self-sufficiency work on the human mind exactly opposite to humility and self-surrender. This is why when we try to control ourselves and fail, we try harder the next time. All human effort expended to be patient will never produce the fruit of patience. A strong enough motivation may produce an appearance of patience—salesmen often do this. Customers may be completely fooled, for the public image is often quite different from what one is at home.

Our problem seems to be that pride takes the way of expediency. It can appear to be humble, teachable, calm, even patient.

> "Some of us have a nervous temperament, and are naturally as quick as a flash to think and act; but let no one think that he cannot learn to become patient. Patience is a plant that will make rapid growth if carefully cultivated."[5]

Cultivation is a process that removes anything that hinders the growth of the plant that is desired. The removal process is not the problem with most of us. It is the failure to be willing to admit what needs to be removed from the character, and to be willing to turn it over to the Lord for Him to remove. If patience is to make rapid growth, there must be a sincere self-examination and willingness to face up to the true facts. "It was on the point where he thought himself strong that Peter was weak; and not until he discerned his weakness could he realize his need of dependence upon Christ."[6]

Patience can take on another cloak we should examine.

> "There are many who, when they are reproved, think it praiseworthy if they receive the rebuke without becoming impatient; but how few take reproof with gratitude of heart, and bless those who seek to save them from pursuing an evil course."[7]

Obviously, patience reaches into areas that we have thought little about. It requires more than refraining from retaliation. Patience seeks to look at every situation or person in the best light possible.

Read Hebrews 11 and catch a vision of the cloud of witnesses from Abel to Samuel and on to an army of unnamed men and women who, through Christ, vanquished Satan and his hosts of evil angels. Then catch the picture of yourself in chapter 12 as Paul says, " . . . let us lay aside every weight . . . "—that is every hindrance. Cultivate out every weed and break up the hard ground. He then speaks of " . . . the sin which doth so easily beset us . . ." Hebrews 12:1. Here we have the old habits that are still with us from the old nature that Satan uses so often.

> "Selfishness and pride will make a stand against anything that would show them to be sinful. We cannot, of ourselves, conquer the evil desires and habits that strive for the mastery. We cannot overcome the mighty foe who holds us in his thrall. God alone can give us the victory . . . But He cannot work in us without our consent and co-operation."[8]

Having done all this, then we can " . . . run with patience the race that is set before us, looking unto Jesus the author and finisher of our faith . . ." Hebrews 12:1,2.

James was one of the sons of thunder. With John, his brother, he would have called fire down from heaven to destroy those who did not readily accept Jesus and the disciples into their city. Jesus, however, was able to change all this so that James knew of the perfect work of patience and left us this counsel, " . . . let patience have her perfect work, that ye may be perfect and entire, wanting nothing." James 1:4.

Notes:
1 The Acts of the Apostles, p. 532.
2 My Life Today, p. 253.
3 My Life Today, p. 248.
4 Christ's Object Lessons, p. 154.
5 My Life Today, p. 97.
6 The Desire of Ages, p. 382.
7 Patriarchs and Prophets, p. 667.
8 Thoughts from the Mount of Blessing, p. 142.

13.

No STOPPING PLACE

The lesson that "true greatness consists in true goodness" has always been difficult to learn.[1] Even the proud monarch Nebuchadnezzar had to learn the hard way. It is so natural, when striving to do right, to feel that we have achieved a degree of godliness through doing good things.

> "The reason many in this age of the world make no greater advancement in the divine life is because they interpret the will of God to be just what they will to do. While following their own desires, they flatter themselves that they are conforming to God's will. These have no conflict with self. There are others who for a time are successful in the struggle against their selfish desire for pleasure and ease. They are sincere and earnest, but grow weary of protracted effort, of daily death, of ceaseless turmoil. Indolence seems inviting, death to self repulsive; and they close their drowsy eyes, and fall under the power of temptation instead of resisting it."[2]

There are two classes pictured in the foregoing paragraph. The first we could classify as permissive believers. These have no, or at the most little, conflict with self. To these it seems easier to delete sanctification from God's gift of righteousness by faith than to follow the Master's invitation, " . . . If any man will come after me, let him deny himself, and take up his cross, and follow me." Matthew 16:24.

The other class are stony ground believers who grow weary because their root is not wholly secure in Christ. They have not learned the joy of renouncing self and of letting Christ carry the load. They have never discovered that His yoke is easy and His burden is light.

Sanctification, as a process, reaches deeper and deeper into our lives and requires total surrender at each step. This, of course, is not easy for the proud heart to find joy in doing.[3]

> "John and Judas are representatives of those who profess to be Christ's followers .... Each possessed serious defects of character; and each had access to the divine grace that transforms character ... One, daily dying to self and overcoming sin, was sanctified through the truth; the other, resisting the transforming power of grace and indulging selfish desires, was brought into bondage to Satan."[4]

Since life is a continuous round of making decisions, it follows logically that this is the area where this daily dying to self must start. Like Jesus, our true Pattern, our automatic response in every decision must be "not my will but Thine be done." This must be more than a verbalization of the thought. It requires a willingness—as God directs—to change, drop, or carry out any plan or desire, no matter how cherished it might be. It requires an acquaintance with, and a sensitivity to, God's will as revealed in Inspiration; we must also be tuned to the still small voice of conscience and carefully evaluate His providential leading.[5]

By following this process the grace of God will "attract the mind upward and habituate it to meditate upon pure and holy things."[6] God-like-ness *is not doing what Christ did, but living the way He lived.* We need to understand clearly Paul's counsel for holy living as described in Colossians 3:3,4. "For ye are dead, and your life is hid with Christ in God. When Christ, who is our life, shall appear, then shall ye also appear with him in glory." What glory is Paul concerned about? "To whom God would make known what is the riches of the glory of this mystery among the Gentiles; which is Christ in you, the hope of glory." Colossians 1:27.

What a privilege that we can be used of God to reveal His own character to an unbelieving world. "Jesus revealed no qualities, and exercised no powers, that men may not have through faith in Him. His perfect humanity is that which all His followers may possess, if they will be in subjection to God as He was."[7]

This is true godliness, not trying to *be good* or *doing good* things but daily dying to self—*truly trusting God*. "My son, give me thine heart, and let thine eyes observe my ways." Proverbs 23:26. We would be amazed at what God would do in our lives if we would stop *trying* and start *dying*—being in subjection to God as Jesus was.

There is, however, a real hindering factor we must face as we attempt to take this step—compromise. This is one of Satan's most effective weapons to keep the Christian from making the spiritual progress God desires him to make. Jesus' life showed no compromise at any time. He was wholly dedicated to do His Father's will. His words, "I delight to do thy will, O my God . . ." Psalms 40:8 reflect the only attitude that is God-like, or acceptable, in God's sight. Reluctant obedience is not obedience at all.

> "When the requirements of God are accounted a burden because they cut across human inclination, we may know that the life is not a Christian life. True obedience is the outworking of a principle within. It springs from the love of righteousness, the love of the law of God. The essence of all righteousness is loyalty to our Redeemer."[8]

The disciples of old, the reformers, and God's people in all ages have met Satan's temptation to compromise their loyalty to God. It is often in what we consider our *strength* that Satan finds our *weakness*. Let us look again at another side of Peter's experience.

> "It was on the point where he thought himself strong that Peter was weak; and not until he discerned his *weakness* could he realize his need of dependence upon Christ. Had he learned the lesson that Jesus sought to teach him in that experience on the sea, he would not have failed when the great test came to him."[9]

Now we can better understand Christ's words to Paul in 2 Corinthians 12:9, " . . . My grace is sufficient for thee; for My strength is made perfect in weakness . . . " Then, as Paul gives answer in the next verse, ". . . for when I am weak, then am I strong." We can see the only way to godliness is by daily dying to self. No, there is no stopping place here. This round of the ladder only opens our eyes to the great vistas ahead as Christ's indwelling becomes the practical key to God-like-ness.

Notes:
1 Prophets and Kings, p. 521.
2 The Acts of the Apostles, p. 565.
3 Christ Our Righteousness, pp. 33, 34.
4 The Acts of the Apostles, pp. 558, 559.
5 Messages to Young People, p. 156.
6 Testimonies, vol. 2, pp. 478, 479.
7 The Desire of Ages, p. 664.
8 Christ's Object Lessons, p. 97.
9 The Desire of Ages, p. 382. (Italics supplied.)

14.

What,
NO MORE COMPETITION?

Did it ever seem strange to you that in God's plan we must recognize that only through godliness can we really have brotherly kindness? If we accept this Biblical principle, we are then face to face with a problem. Who is my brother? Jesus answers this in Luke 8:21, " . . . My mother and my brethren are these which hear the word of God, and do it." It is quite evident here that Jesus is not limiting "brethren" to those who perfectly obeyed the Word, but those who were *desiring* to obey. Matthew 12:49 tells us that as He spoke these words He was pointing to His disciples who were a long way from doing all that the Word had spoken. Competition was a continuous problem in each of them.

The spirit that promotes competitive thinking is the spirit of judging. The spirit of competition and of judging, from which it springs, are both of Satan and can only serve his purposes. Then, how can we truly be free from these hindering factors? Again, Jesus gives us the answer. His life was a perfect demonstration of how we are to live in relation to our brothers and sisters. In chapter three we referred to the quotation found in <u>Thoughts from the Mount of Blessing</u>, p. 71. We will quote it here again for it contains the answer to how Jesus' life was filled with brotherly kindness, even to those who treated Him with contempt.[1]

"The Father's presence encircled Christ, and nothing befell Him but that which infinite love permitted for the blessing of the world.   Here was His source of comfort, and it is for us.   He who is imbued with the Spirit of Christ abides in Christ. The blow that is aimed at him falls upon the Saviour, who surrounds him with His presence.   Whatever comes to him comes from Christ.   He has no need to resist evil, for Christ is his defense.   Nothing can touch him except by our Lord's permission, and 'all things' that are permitted 'work together for good to them that love God.'   Romans 8:28."[2]

By Christ accepting everything that happened in His life as coming directly from the Father's hand, even though it originated with Satan, He had true peace.   He was able to accept the worst abuse it was possible for any human being to experience, both mental and physical, yet treat with utmost kindness the human instrument through which it came.   In fact, it was this that kept Him from seeing people as responsible for what they did to Him.   He constantly looked beyond the human and saw Satan as the real enemy.   This enabled Him to empathize with even His persecutors and treat them with brotherly kindness. He pitied *them* instead of *Himself.*   He constantly tried to excuse His followers because of their ignorance.   He knew that Satan was blinding them.

We are told that His source of comfort is also ours.   Can you see what would happen in God's family if His brethren lived by the same policy He lived by as a human being here on earth?   Brotherly kindness can come in no other way. We can not force ourselves to be kind and loving.   It must be from inside– from the heart.   Jesus' plan is the only way the heart can truly respond impartially for the eyes are then no longer focused upon men or their unkind acts.

The real test is found in the "*all* things" of Romans 8:28. We are quite ready to apply Christ's method in our lives to *some* things, but does it really mean *everything*?   Yes, there are no exceptions.   He is either Lord of all or not at all.

God is so careful to protect us that He will turn every evil thrust Satan can hurl at us into a blessing if we accept the "all things" as a practical working principle in our lives.

> "The trials of life are God's workmen, to remove the impurities and roughness from our character. Their hewing, squaring, and chiseling, their burnishing and polishing, is a painful process; it is hard to be pressed down to the grinding wheel. But the stone is brought forth prepared to fill its place in the heavenly temple. Upon no useless material does the Master bestow such careful, thorough work. Only His precious stones are polished after the similitude of a palace."[3]

Here is another very practical reason to believe, accept, and apply the Scriptures in daily living. If the "all things" includes both the good and the bad experiences of life, then Paul's words in 1 Thessalonians 5:18, "In everything give thanks: for this is the will of God in Christ Jesus concerning you," become very practical to us in our daily living. Jesus lived this way and if we are to be successful in our Christian life, we must follow His example. This does not mean that we must enjoy everything that happens to us, but we must give thanks to God—yes, even rejoice. Jesus did not enjoy the mistreatment of men acting as demons, but He knew that the world would be blessed thereby. We will not enjoy the "all things" that happen to us, but we can be thankful! We can thank Him for seeing something in us worth working upon. We are the material that, when polished, will be fit for His palace and every stone will have its place and be contented therewith. All competition will be gone forever, for the spirit of judging, pride and selfishness will be eradicated with their originator.

Notes:
1 The Desire of Ages, p. 87.
2 Thoughts from the Mount of Blessing, p. 71.
3 Thoughts from the Mount of Blessing, p. 10.

15.

Love UNLIMITED

Add to brotherly kindness charity, or divine love. God's plan has never changed. He will bring man back to the place where the uninhibited, divine love of God will flow through him. This will surpass the experience of Adam when he came forth from the hand of God. It was this that Jesus prayed for in His last prayer for His disciples before he went to Gethsemane, " . . . that the love wherewith thou has loved me may be in them, and I in them." John 17:26. Imagine, if you can, divine love flowing through human channels.

The goal of sanctification is to systematically produce this love in man. It is not accomplished by *trying* to be loving but by *dying* to self and to the hindering factors that inhibit, or prevent, God from doing His work in our lives.

All the way up this ladder the process has been the same. The last step is to taste of the greatest power in heaven or upon earth—that of divine love. The hindering factor is Satan's counterfeit of God's love—human emotion. There will be human emotion in response to divine love but it is a response, not the love itself.

> "The church is God's appointed agency for the salvation of men. It was organized for service, and its mission is to carry the gospel to the world . . . The church is the repository of the riches of the grace of Christ; and through the church *will* eventually be made manifest, even to 'the principalities and pow-

> ers in heavenly places,' (Ephesians 3:10) the final
> and full display of the love of God."[1]

If this is to happen in these closing days of earth's history, we had better know what this love is and how it can be revealed through human beings.

Divine love is a principle that governs heaven and the entire universe, with the exception of this earth. It is a principle of action, a principle of life. Divine love is like a two way street: it flows from God in both directions so that we are without excuse—first, in His being willing to take time to patiently deal with the rebel angel Lucifer, instead of meting out justice when it was due. This kindness was primarily to enable His created beings to understand what divine love really is—to give them an opportunity to use their will (the power of choice) intelligently. In the final decision about one-third of the angels of heaven decided against God.

The mental agony of God in sustaining such a loss, and the subsequent confusion in the minds of loyal angels and beings on other planets, caused Him to put into effect His marvelous plan of redemption. God's love is more fully revealed when we understand that "from the beginning God and Christ knew of the apostasy of Satan, and of the fall of man through the deceptive power of the apostate."[2] While God did not plan these emergencies, He foresaw them and then devised a plan to use them to implant His love forever in the hearts of His created beings.

So comprehensive is His plan of redemption that He actually built it around the incarnation. Jesus Christ, the Son of God, became man so that the human family and all of God's creation would have a perfect pattern to guide them forever as this divine love would flow back to God. This is the second great demonstration of His love.

While this plan provides a legal basis for man's salvation, it also provides the example for every Christian to follow, which enables God's love to flow through them. Jesus said, "For I came down from heaven, not to do mine own will, but the will of him that sent me." John 6:38. Paul said, "I am crucified with Christ: nevertheless I live; yet not I, but Christ liveth in me: and the life which I now live in the flesh I live by the faith of the Son of God, who loved me, and gave himself for me." Galatians 2:20. " . . . They that are Christ's have crucified the flesh with the affections and lusts." Galatians 5:24.

There is no other plan that will enable the uninhibited love of God to flow through human beings. In order for the human vessel to be a clear channel, self must be crucified. Any trace elements of self, willingly left, will mar the image and prevent the church from giving to the universe "the final and full display of the love of God."

Sanctification will have accomplished its work in our lives when we can honestly say in every experience in life, "Not my will but Thine be done." This is, indeed, love unlimited.

Notes:
1 <u>The Acts of the Apostles</u>, p. 9 (Italics supplied.)
2 <u>Patriarchs and Prophets</u>, p. 22.

16.

WAS JESUS *Tempted* JUST LIKE WE ARE?

"For we have not an high priest which cannot be touched with the feelings of our infirmities; but was in all points tempted like as we are, yet without sin." Hebrews 4:15. This verse of Scripture has been, and still is, the basis for a great deal of unhealthy discussion regarding the human nature of Christ. There are some who claim Jesus had to be tempted in the identical manner as every human being has been tempted in order to meet the requirements of this text. This conclusion is arrived at without taking into account all that God has revealed to His church on the subject.

If Jesus was tempted to steal, lie, swear, be impure in thought or deed, he resisted that temptation in one of two ways: (1) by resisting the inclination to yield or (2) by realizing that He was helpless and turning the problem over to His Father. In either case He would have had to have a propensity, or inclination, for Satan to appeal to. Yet, Jesus said, "Hereafter I will not talk much with you: for the prince of this world cometh, and hath found nothing in me." John 14:30. This was very close to the end of Jesus' life on earth. Satan had probed into every corner of Christ's life and could find nothing to build any temptation upon.

> "Not even by a thought could Christ be brought to yield to the power of his subtle temptations. Satan finds in human hearts some point where he can

gain a foothold—some sinful desire is cherished by means of which his temptations assert their power."[1]

Remember, it was as a human being that Jesus met these temptations. "Not a single thought or feeling responded to temptation."[2] Notice, there was no response by either thought or feeling which must precede a temptation. "Every sin, every discord, every defiling lust that transgression had brought, was torture to His spirit."[3] "Never, in any way, leave the slightest impression upon human minds that a taint of, or *inclination* to, corruption rested upon Christ, or that He in any way yielded to corruption."[4] "As the sinless One, His nature recoiled from evil."[5]

Our text being considered says, " . . . [He] was tempted in all points like as we are . . . " and this is true. In order to find the answer to the "how" question, let us look at another quotation about our Lord.

> "It was a difficult task for the Prince of life to carry out the plan which He had undertaken for the salvation of man, in clothing His divinity with humanity. He had received honor in the heavenly courts, and was familiar with absolute power. It was *as difficult* for Him to keep the *level of humanity* as for man to rise above the low level of their depraved natures, and be *partakers of the divine nature*."[6]

"To keep *His glory veiled* as the child of a fallen race, this was the most severe discipline to which the Prince of life could subject Himself."[7] This is where we all have our difficulties. It is a problem for us to let the divine nature of Christ be reflected in us.

Let us analyze what this quotation is telling us. It was extremely difficult for Christ to clothe His *divinity with humanity*. Why? "Jesus revealed *no qualities*, and *exercised no powers*, that *men may not have through faith in Him*. His perfect humanity is that which all His followers may possess, if they will be in subjection to God as He was."[8]

Jesus said, "I can of mine own self do nothing . . . " John 5:30.

It is quite clear that when Christ "laid aside His royal robe and kingly crown,"[9] He took upon Him the nature of man "*as God created him.*" "Christ came to the earth, taking humanity and standing as man's representative, to show in the controversy with Satan that man, *as God created him*, connected with the Father and the Son could obey every divine requirement."[10] "*He began where the first Adam began.*"[11] Christ, as the second Adam, must succeed where the first Adam failed, using only the same power the first Adam had available to him. "When Adam was assailed by the tempter in Eden he was without the taint of sin . . . Christ, in the wilderness of temptation, stood in Adam's place to bear the test he failed to endure."[12]

There is no evidence in the Word of God that sinful nature can ever be obedient to God! The message of God to man is that he *inherently* has a sinful carnal nature which is unredeemable.

> "The inheritance of children is that of sin. Sin has separated them from God. Jesus gave His life that He might unite the broken links to God. As related to the first Adam, men receive from him nothing but guilt and the sentence of death."[13]

"Because the carnal mind is enmity (hatred) against God: *for it is not subject to the law of God, neither indeed can be.*" Romans 8:7. (Italics supplied.) Christ never tried to show to anyone that *sinful nature* could become *sinless nature.* His message was always, " . . . Ye must be born again." John 3:7. " . . . Except a corn of wheat fall into the ground and die, it abideth alone . . . " John 12:24. " . . . Are ye able to drink of the cup that I shall drink of, and to be baptized with the baptism that I am baptized with? . . ." Matthew 20:22.

If Christ had sinless nature how could He be tempted like I am? What is temptation? "Temptation is resisted when man is powerfully influenced to do a wrong action and, knowing that he can do it, resists, by faith, with a firm hold upon divine power."[14] Temptation only exists when there is a "powerful influence to do a wrong action." "But every man is tempted when he is drawn away of his own lust, and enticed." James 1:14. How could Christ be tempted to do an evil thing when "the refined sensibilities of His holy nature rendered contact with evil unspeakably painful to Him"?[15] Christ hated sin with a perfect hatred. His Spirit, indwelling man, is the only power that brings man to hate sin, which every born-again Christian must learn to do.

Christ, in order to be tempted as we are, must have had a strong desire to do a wrong act, but resisted by trusting in His Father. How could Satan find something that would fit these criteria? Satan learned, even when Christ was a child, that it was useless to try to tempt Him to retaliate. Even when abused, to be irritated, angered, or to do any *bad thing* was unthinkable to Him.

> "Of the bitterness that falls to the lot of humanity, there was no part that Christ did not taste. There were those who tried to cast contempt upon Him because of His birth, and even in His childhood He had to meet their scornful looks and evil whisperings. If He had responded by an impatient word or look, if He had conceded to His brothers by even one wrong act, He would have failed of being a perfect example. Thus He would have failed of carrying out the plan for our redemption."[16]

Satan knows how difficult it is for man to live here as a born-again Christian, keeping his natural sinful nature crucified. He knows that it takes a daily dying to self (1 Corinthians 15:31)—even a continuous crucifixion of habits from that old, but natural, nature. 2 Corinthians 4:10-12. Therefore, he switched his approach to Christ, tempting Him to reveal *His natural nature*, which He had laid aside when He came to this earth. To reveal His natural divine nature would have ruined the plan of salvation, for Christ must use only that which is available to man.

Never had there been born a sinless human being until Christ was born of Mary. Never has there been born one since. Satan's experience in dealing with *sinful* babies, children, youth or adults was of no value when dealing with *sinless* human nature. He tried in every way possible to force Christ to reveal His *natural divine nature*. Realizing that Christ's greatest problem while here on earth was to be *accepted as the Messiah* (the anointed One), Satan would use *this natural desire* and try through temptations to get Him to take Himself out of His Father's hands and respond by using His own divine nature that He had laid aside. From His childhood to Calvary this one goal was never given up by Satan. His temptations become more powerful until at the cross the challenge was hurled at Him for hours, "If you are the Christ come down and we will believe." Christ, knowing that He could respond at any time and compel His tormentors to acknowledge Him as Lord and King, refused. He trusted His present and future life to His Father's hands.

> "Thus when Christ was treated with contempt, there came to Him *a strong temptation* to manifest His divine character. By a word, by a look, He could compel His persecutors to confess that He was Lord above kings and rulers, priests and temple. But it was *His difficult task* to keep to the position He had chosen as one with humanity."[17]

What a temptation! No human could ever be tempted like He was!

How was He tempted as we are? The born-again Christian must die to *his old natural nature*, which is *sinful*. "They that are Christ's have crucified the flesh with the affections and lusts." Galatians 5:24. This is stated over and over in God's Word. Selfishness is declared to be the root of all evil.[18] In the judgement all sins come under the heading of selfishness.[19] "What is the sign of a new heart? A changed life. There is a daily, hourly dying to selfishness and pride."[20] It would have shown *selfishness* for Christ to act at any time *on His own desires*.

Let your mind probe to its greatest depths and you will find that all sin is selfishness! It is for this reason that when Satan tempts the born-again Christian to do a wrong thing, the old nature, which he has crucified, still seems to urge him to do it. How can this be when the old nature is crucified? Here is where Satan's method of working is revealed. Satan takes advantage of the fact that the born-again Christian, who has a new *nature* given to him at justification, does not receive a new *character* in the same way. A character still has to be developed. This was true with Adam and it is still true with all of the human family. God created Adam perfect in every way, but he had to develop a perfect character, which he failed to do. This is where Christ succeeded and Adam failed. Christ then credits to the born-again Christian's account His own sinless character. This is *placed* to the *account* of the Christian who accepts this as a fact and then allows Christ to begin the work of sanctification, which is God *changing* his *character* so that it will reflect the *character* that is *legally credited* to him in justification.

What does this have to do with how Satan tempts us? Let us take a look at what character really is. "The character is revealed, not by occasional good deeds and occasional misdeeds, but by the tendency of the habitual words and acts."[21] Habits, then, make up our *character*. So, when we live with a sinful nature controlling us, the *habits* that we form reflect that *sinful nature*.

Habits or character cannot be given instantaneously; that is why "there is no such thing as instantaneous sanctification."[22] With the *old habits* still alive in the newborn Christian, even though they are being worked on by Christ, we can see how Satan sets the trap. He knows that he has no power to bring back to life the *old nature*, and Christ *will not* bring it back, so Satan's only hope is through the habits. He sets that trap, which may be through people or circumstances, so the natural response is a *habitual* response. Then he blames us for responding, and uses our habitual response as proof that the *old nature* is not dead after all. He hopes in this way to force us into discouragement and to get us to *give up and turn away from Christ*, thinking that the whole plan is not working. It is thus that we resurrect the *old nature*. Only then can Satan take *control* again.

Can you see that Satan is tempting the Christian in exactly the same way he tempted Christ? In both cases he is trying to force the tempted ones to reveal their *natural natures*. The difference is that our *natural nature* is wicked, so we do not want to reveal it. Christ's *natural nature* was *divine*, so He *desired* to reveal it. But *both* must rely on *surrender to divine control—Christ to His Father and us to Christ*. Christ's surrender led Him to Calvary and apparent defeat from every human viewpoint. Our surrender leads us to eternal life and peace with God.

Selfishness, the root, is the target. But there is one vast difference between Christ's temptation and ours. If we fail, " . . . we have an advocate with the Father, Jesus Christ the righteous." 1 John 2:1. If Jesus had failed, *all* would have been lost! The *entire* plan of redemption would have failed and Satan would have triumphed.

Yes, " . . . [He] was tempted in all points like as we are, yet without sin." Hebrews 4:5.

Notes:

1   The Review and Herald, November 8, 1887.
2   Testimonies, vol. 5, p. 422.
3   The Desire of Ages, p. 111.
4   The SDA Bible Commentary, Vol. 5, pp. 1128, 1129,
    Letter 8, 1895. (Italics supplied.)
5   Testimonies, vol. 2, p. 202.
6   The SDA Bible Commentary, Vol. 7, p. 930,
    The Review and Herald, April 1, 1875
    (Italics supplied.)
7   The SDA Bible Commentary, vol. 5, p. 1081, Letter
    19, 1901. (Italics supplied.)
8   The Desire of Ages, p. 664. (Italics supplied.)
9   The Review and Herald, June 15, 1905.
10 Signs of the Times, June 9, 1898. (Italics supplied.)
11 The Youth's Instructor, June 2, 1898. (Italics sup-
    plied.)
12 The Review and Herald, July 28, 1874.
13 Child Guidance, p. 475.
14 The SDA Bible Commentary, vol. 5, p. 1082,
    The Youth's Instructor, July 20, 1899.
15 The SDA Bible Commentary, vol 7A, p. 451,
    The Review and Herald, November 8, 1887.
16 The Desire of Ages, p. 88.
17 The Desire of Ages, p. 700. (Italics supplied.)
18 Child Guidance, p. 294.
19 Testimony Treasures, vol. 1, p. 518.
20 The Youth's Instructor, September 26, 1901.
21 Steps to Christ, pp. 57, 58.
22 The Sanctified Life, p. 10.

17.

FOLLOW *Me*

"Then said Jesus unto his disciples, If any man will come after me, let him deny himself, and take up his cross, and follow me." Matthew 16:24.

> "Jesus now explained to His disciples that His own life of self-abnegation was an example of what theirs should be. Calling about Him, with the disciples, the people who had been lingering near, He said, 'If any man will come after Me, let him deny himself, and take up his cross daily, and follow Me.' The cross was associated with the power of Rome. It was the instrument of the most cruel and humiliating form of death. The lowest criminals were required to bear the cross to the place of execution; and often as it was about to be laid upon their shoulders, they resisted with desperate violence, until they were overpowered, and the instrument of torture was bound upon them. But Jesus bade His followers take up the cross and bear it after Him. To the disciples His words, though dimly comprehended, pointed to their submission to the most bitter humiliation,—submission even unto death for the sake of Christ. No more complete self-surrender could the Saviour's words have pictured."[1]

You will notice that Luke adds another dimension with the word "daily." Webster defines abnegation as "surrender" or "relinquish." When we realize this surrender is even unto death, it takes on a very significant meaning, especially when coupled with the word "daily." It sounds strangely familiar, for it was Paul who said, "I die daily." 1 Corinthians 15:31, and again, "Always bearing about in the body the dying of the Lord Jesus, that the life also of Jesus might be made manifest in our body. For we which live are always delivered unto death for Jesus' sake, that the life also of Jesus might be made manifest in our mortal flesh. So then death worketh in us, but life in you." 2 Corinthians 4:10-12.

Obviously, there is only one way to reflect the image of Jesus and that is not by trying but by dying. Since this is made so clear in the Scriptures, Satan has fought this principle with all his power. He has focused our attention on Christ's words and emphasized the word "deny." However, he has made us think that denying self is the same as self-denial. By the simple act of reversing the order of the two words, the meaning is completely changed in the human mind.

To practice self-denial can be a real beneficial experience in the character building process. This must never be equated with denying self, which is the process of crucifying self and keeping self crucified. When Christ is enthroned in the heart, self is dethroned; and when self is enthroned, Christ is dethroned. Every decision we make must be made by using the same formula that Christ used, "Not my will but Thine." The Saviour followed this practice so completely that He said, " . . . The words that I speak unto you I speak not of myself: but the Father that dwelleth in me, he doeth the works." John 14:10.

It is this secret that Paul learned and passed on to Timothy as the foundation of our life with Christ here and now. He said, "It is a faithful saying: For if we be dead with Him, we shall also live with Him." 2 Timothy 2:11.

Jesus not only said that we must deny self, but also take up our cross. It is an amazing fact that Christ uses the cross as the agent to bind the believer to Himself.

"The yoke and the cross are symbols represent-ing the same thing,—*the giving up of the will to God.* Wearing the yoke unites finite man in a com-panionship with the dearly beloved Son of God. Lifting the cross cuts away self from the soul, and places man where he learns how to bear Christ's burdens. *We cannot follow Christ* without wearing His yoke, without lifting the cross and bearing it after Him."[2]

"*We cannot retain self and yet enter the kingdom of God.* If we ever attain unto holiness, it will be through the renunciation of self and the reception of the mind of Christ."[3]

"The reason many in this age of the world make no greater advancement in the divine life is because they interpret the will of God to be just what they will to do. While following their own desires, they flatter themselves that they are conforming to God's will. These have no conflicts with self. There are others who for a time are successful in the struggle against their selfish desire for pleasure and ease. They are sincere and earnest, but grow weary of protracted effort, of daily death, of ceaseless tur-moil. Indolence seems inviting, death to self repul-sive; and they close their drowsy eyes, and fall un-der the power of temptation instead of resisting it."[4]

Christ's emphatic statement, "follow Me," is utterly im-possible unless we experience that which goes before in the same verse. He was not urging His disciples and fol-lowers to *do* what He did but to *live* as He lived.

The Father did, through Christ, that which He sent Him into the world to do. This was made possible by Christ choosing, every moment of His life, to be as the clay in His Father's hands. In His sphere this surrender brought the only hope of peace to a universe that had been thrown into confusion by the rebellion of Lucifer who became Satan. In our sphere this surrender brings the only hope of our personal salvation. It is our privilege to live a life here which He can use as a magnetic force to persuade men and women of *God's plan of salvation*. This plan is, indeed, the only process conceivable that can prepare human beings to live eternally in the perfect environment of the home of the saved.

"Implicit belief in Christ's word is true humility, true self-surrender."[5] "Self-surrender is the substance of the teachings of Christ."[6] It is only as we see the importance of trusting Christ perfectly, even though all things seem impossible, that we can grasp the urgency of Christ's words to Nicodemus, "Ye must be born again."

We had no choice in our first birth, but the new birth depends entirely upon our exercising the free will that can only be kept free by our choosing to die to self and letting Christ reign within.

Matthew closes his gospel by quoting the words of Jesus, ". . . All power [authority, *exousia*] is given unto me in heaven and in earth." Matthew 28:18. This was the Father's response to His Son for a life of total surrender while here on earth as He lived in the human flesh that He had assumed.

Christ was offered short cut routes. In the wilderness, at the very beginning of His public ministry, Satan tried to bargain with Him. After showing Him all the kingdoms of this world and the glory of them, Satan said, " . . . All these things will I give Thee, if Thou wilt fall down and worship me." Matthew 4:9. What a short cut! But by choosing to believe and trust God, even though it was by the way of the cross, and a willingness to die, He received from His Father *all power in heaven and in earth*. We must keep in mind that Christ made this choice in human flesh with *no power that is not available to each of us*.

"Jesus revealed no qualities, and exercised no powers, that men may not have through faith in Him. His perfect humanity is that which all His followers may possess, if they will be in subjection to God as He was."[7]

Probably the most subtle short cut Satan offered to Jesus was at the beginning of the wilderness experience.

"He [Satan] tried to make Christ believe that God did not require Him to pass through self-denial and the sufferings He anticipated; that he had been sent from heaven to bear to Him the message that God only designed to prove His willingness to endure.

"Satan told Christ that He was only to set His feet in the bloodstained path, but not to travel it. He also stated that he was the angel that stayed the hand of Abraham as the knife was raised to slay Isaac, and he had now come to save His life; that it was not necessary for Him to endure the painful hunger and death from starvation; he would help Him bear a part of the work in the plan of salvation."[8]

Satan has come to every child of Adam, since the beginning, with the same message, "Christ died for you so that you do not have to die." It sounds so good because it is a partial truth. Christ *did die* to deliver us from the *wages of sin,* which is *eternal death.* However, He also lived a life of total self-abnegation (relinquishment) as an example of what ours must be. Satan will try to bring every kind of short cut to the struggling Christian, but the only route to the kingdom of God is in following Jesus.

Notes:

1 The Desire of Ages p. 416-17.
2 The SDA Bible Commentary, vol. 5, pp. 1090-91,
   The Review and Herald, October 23, 1900. (Italics
   supplied.)
3 Thoughts from the Mount of Blessing, p. 143. (Italics
   supplied.)
4 The Acts of the Apostles, p. 565.
5 The Desire of Ages, p. 535.
6 The Desire of Ages, p. 523.
7 The Desire of Ages, p. 644. (Italics supplied.)
8 Selected Messages, book 1, p. 273.

18.

ABIDE IN

The thirteenth chapter of John pictures for us the Passover supper as celebrated by Jesus and His disciples the night before the crucifixion. During this supper one of the twelve disciples would depart, never to walk again with them. Judas would even betray his Lord thinking he was promoting the kingdom of God on earth. During the meal Jesus had told them He was going away and that they would not be able to follow Him. As usual, Peter asked the questions they all, no doubt, were thinking: "Where are you going and why cannot I follow you?" Then follows a sincere commitment, "I will lay down my life for thy sake." John 13:37. Peter and the disciples would make other commitments this same night.

Mark 14:30,31 reads, "And Jesus saith unto him, [Peter] Verily I say unto thee, That this day, even in this night, before the cock crow twice, thou shalt deny me thrice. But he [Peter] spake the more vehemently, If I should die with thee, I will not deny thee in any wise. *Likewise also said they all.*" (Italics supplied.)

Jesus knew that the response from these men was sincere, but the flesh was weak. Their own failures would be Satan's most effective weapon to discourage them. In order to counteract this inevitable experience Jesus gave them the beautiful message of John 14.

At the conclusion of His message we find the simple expression: "Let us go hence." Jesus knew where He was going. The disciples only desired to be with Him so they followed. It was night and the city streets were, no doubt, filled with people for this was the time of the Passover celebration. At these seasons the hills were dotted with tents, for there was not enough lodging in the city for the throngs that attended on these feast days.

Jesus and His disciples left the upper room and went into the busy street. He led the way toward a familiar spot that was very dear to Him—the Mount of Olives. This was not His destination, but He took advantage of a flourishing grapevine to give one more lesson to these men whom He loved so dearly.

The moon was shining upon this vine when Jesus stopped and fastened His eyes upon it. No doubt each disciple also looked at the vine. Then the words came clear and forceful, breaking the stillness of the night, "I am the true vine, and my Father is the husbandman." John 15:1. I can hear Peter as he may have turned to John and said, "Did you hear what He said? I don't understand, everyone knows that Israel is the vine!" John may have responded by saying, "I don't understand either, but let's listen. He may explain it." Jesus went on with the lesson.

"Every branch in me that beareth not fruit he [My Father] taketh away; and every branch that beareth fruit, he [My Father] purgeth it, that it may bring forth more fruit." John 15:2.

The terms "vine," "branch," "husbandman," "purgeth," etc. were all familiar terms, for vineyards were common in that area. The disciples understood that the purging was done with a pruning knife. No doubt, the message that a branch not bearing fruit would be cut off completely, and if it was bearing it would still be cut but not so severely, was clear to these men, even if it did not fit into their scheme of thinking. The Jews certainly did not need such severe treatment! They were Israelites—children of Abraham! For many generations they had been in the vine until, in their minds, they were the vine itself.

Jesus attempted to encourage these men by saying, "Now ye are clean through the word which I have spoken unto you." John 15:3. These words can be best understood in the light of other Scriptures such as, "Let the word of Christ dwell in you richly . . ." Colossians 3:16. "Wherefore lay apart all filthiness and superfluity of naughtiness, and receive with meekness the engrafted word, which is able to save your souls. But be ye doers of the word, and not hearers only, deceiving your own selves." James 1:21,22. Christ was really saying, "Ye are clean through believing the word which I have spoken unto you."

The real burden on the heart of Christ is made clear in the next verse: "Abide in me, and I in you . . . " John 15:4. It is clear that the Master is looking forward to His trial and crucifixion when even His disciples would forsake Him. He urged upon them facts that they had not seen as yet. " . . . As the branch cannot bear fruit of itself, except it abide in the vine; no more can ye, except ye abide in me." John 15:4. It is still true today; we are helpless unless we abide in Him. Even though things seem impossible and all is failing, the message is the same: "Abide in me; trust me."

This message of the vine and branches is best understood when coupled with Romans 11. We have here an olive tree instead of a grapevine. Both were symbols of Israel and, as such, were revered by the Jews. The wild olive was a symbol of the Gentiles, and the good olive was a symbol of Israel.

Grafting is the process by which the wild becomes tame and, therefore, useful and good. The process of grafting teaches the basic secret of living the Christian life. Like most things that are worthwhile, we must do a bit of digging to find the truth.

When Romans 11:24 speaks of a wild olive tree and a good olive tree, Paul is referring to the kingdom of Satan and the kingdom of God. The only way a branch from Satan and his kingdom can become a branch in Christ and His kingdom is via the process of grafting.

The Husbandman (Christ) goes looking for a branch (us) that desires to become a part of His kingdom. Christ says, "Ye have not chosen me, but I have chosen you, and ordained you, that ye should go and bring forth fruit . . . " John 15:16. Christ, in His unspeakable love, calls all men but only a few respond to that call by yielding to Him.

Before Christ can do anything toward grafting the branch into Himself, He must prepare the good olive tree to receive the wild branch. Paul says that this is contrary to nature. But, are not most of man's ways contrary to Christ? "For my thoughts are not your thoughts, neither are your ways my ways, saith the Lord." Isaiah 55:8.

Man takes a good branch and grafts it into a wild stalk or root system and thereby produces good fruit. God takes a wild branch and grafts it into a tame root system and produces the very best fruit possible. Man cannot do his work in the way God does His. The whole plan of salvation is God working in His own way in the lives of men and man allowing Him the liberty to do so.

If man does his grafting work the way God does His, the only product is more wild fruit. This, alone, should teach us that our only work is to surrender and trust the Master-Worker. "If ye be willing and obedient, ye shall eat the good of the land:" Isaiah 1:19. The willingness is ours; the obedience, He accomplishes in every trusting soul.

God prepared the good Olive Tree to receive the wild branches at Calvary. But we say, "What about those from Adam to Calvary?" Remember, Christ is " . . . the Lamb slain from the foundation of the world." Revelation 13:8. Every wild branch from Adam until Jesus returns must be grafted in at Calvary.

"The light shining from the cross reveals the love

of God. His love is drawing us to Himself. If we do not resist this drawing, we shall be led to the foot of the cross in repentance for the sins that have crucified the Saviour. Then the Spirit of God through faith produces a new life in the soul. The thoughts and desires are brought into obedience to the will of Christ. The heart, the mind, are created anew in the image of Him who works in us to subdue all things to Himself."[1]

Now that we have been drawn to Calvary, let us see how the Husbandman does His grafting. Like the horticulturist, the Husbandman takes the pruning knife and cuts the willing branch completely free from its former source of life. This initial work is severe and must be done by the Husbandman. Our only part is to desire and be willing for Him to do the work. We must be careful not to complain as to *how* He works.

The good Olive Tree must be wounded in order to receive the branch to be grafted in. That wound was inflicted at Calvary. Now the branch must be shaped to fit into the Calvary wound. "... Everyone who confesses Me by sharing My sacrifice for the lost shall be confessed as a sharer in the glory and joy of the redeemed."[2]

Paul said, "I am crucified with Christ . . . " Galatians 2:20 and, again, " . . . they that are Christ's have crucified the flesh [old nature] with the affections and lusts." Galatians 5:24. When the branch is cut off from its former source of life, it is cut off from its old nature. But the Husbandman does not leave it to die. He carefully puts the branch in the wounded, good Olive Tree. Then He covers the joint with grafting wax (His robe of righteousness). The grafting wax is intended to keep out any infection or disease that would hinder the growth process.

"The Father's presence encircled Christ, and nothing befell Him but that which infinite love permitted for the blessing of the world. Here was His source of comfort, and it is for us. He who is imbued with the Spirit of Christ abides in Christ. The blow that is aimed at him falls upon the Saviour, who surrounds him with His presence. Whatever comes to him comes from Christ. He has no need to resist evil, for Christ is his defense. Nothing can touch him except by our Lord's permission, and 'all things' that are permitted 'work together for good to them that love God.' Romans 8:28."[3]

The Husbandman is still not finished. He then takes strong grafting tape and winds it around the branch and the tree stalk. Layer after layer is applied until the winds and storms of life cannot loosen the branch that is grafted in. The branch must become one with the Olive Tree (or Vine).

> "The connection of the branch with the vine, He said, represents the relation you are to sustain to Me. The scion [branch] is engrafted into the living vine, and fiber by fiber, vein by vein, it grows into the vine stock. The life of the vine becomes the life of the branch."[4]

Even then the Husbandman is not through with the branch, for His purpose for the branch is fruit bearing. ". . . The fruit of the Spirit is love, joy, peace, longsuffering, gentleness, goodness, faith, meekness, temperance . . . " Galatians 5:22,23. This brings us back to the wedding garment again, the robe of Christ's righteousness which is His character, the robe we must all wear in order to be ready for the Lord's return.

In order for this fruit to appear there will have to be some pruning. This is also the work of the Husbandman. There is often an overgrowth that must be cut back to develop strength in the branch. Excessive foliage often gives the wrong impression and hinders the fruit from proper development.

The one thing the Husbandman keeps looking for is the deadly characteristic common to almost all branches—the tendency to droop. The problem is that when the drooping branch touches the ground, it sends out rootlets and then tries to take its nourishment from two sources. But Christ says, "No man can serve two masters . . . " Matthew 6:24.

The pruning knife must be used to cut these rootlets so that the branch will have its life from only one source. With tender care the Husbandman lifts the drooping branch and fastens it to the Trellis where it can breathe the fresh air and bathe in the sunshine of God's love. Every inherited and cultivated tendency to evil is cut away in this pruning process which is called sanctification. This is the work of the Husbandman. The branch is to abide and let the Husbandman do His work as He knows best for each of us.

Only by abiding can we walk in perfection, for that perfection is His, not ours. How appreciative we should be that He allows us to be clothed with His robe of righteousness.

Notes:
1 The Desire of Ages, p. 176.
2 The Desire of Ages, p. 357.
3 Thoughts from the Mount of Blessing, p. 71.
4 The Desire of Ages, p. 675.

APPENDIX A

The Nature OF CHRIST

The human nature of Christ means everything to us and the subject deserves more than just ordinary investigation.

> "When we approach this subject, we would do well to heed the words spoken by Christ to Moses at the burning bush, 'Put off thy shoes from off thy feet, for the place where on thou standest is holy ground.' We should come to this study with the humility of a learner, with a contrite heart. And the study of the incarnation of Christ is a fruitful field, which will repay the searcher who digs deep for hidden truth."[1]

In Hebrews 2:16 we read, "For verily he took not on him the nature of angels; but he took on him the seed of Abraham." A quick analysis of this verse might lead one to rationalize that if Christ took the seed of Abraham, He could not have been the second Adam. However, the whole human family has their roots in Adam, not angels. Paul, whom I believe wrote both Romans and Hebrews, gives us another reason why Christ was the second Adam. Romans 9:6 says, ". . . they are not all Israel, which are of Israel." Verse seven says, " . . . In Isaac shall thy seed be called." Abraham's children, or seed, were to be of promise. In verse eight we read, " . . . the children of the flesh, these are not the children of God: but the children of the promise are counted for the seed." Christ was the Child of promise, the

Son of God. He would, of necessity, be the seed of Abraham as He was born not of the will of the flesh. John 1:13. There are only two origins for man, by the will of the flesh or directly from God. Adam was direct from God as was the second Adam, Jesus Christ.

> "Christ did not make believe take human nature; He did verily take it. He did in reality possess human nature. As the children are partakers of flesh and blood, He also, Himself, likewise took part of the same. He was the son of Mary; He was the seed of David according to human descent."[2]

Yes, Jesus was truly a human being just as much as was Adam, whom He had created. Spiritually, He was the seed of Abraham and, fleshly, the seed of David.

In Romans 8:3 Paul even gets a bit more specific, " . . . God sending his own Son in the *likeness* of sinful flesh . . ." The inspired commentary on this verse says, "As the image made in the *likeness* of the destroying serpents was lifted up for their healing, so One made 'in the *likeness* of sinful flesh' was to be their Redeemer."[3] The people of Israel knew the brazen serpent was not one of the fiery serpents, but it was made in the *likeness* of them. Jesus was made in the *likeness* of His brethren. Man was made in the likeness of God, but he was not God.

To be born of the flesh, according to Jesus when He talked to Nicodemus, was what made it absolutely necessary to have a new birth. John 3:1-6. Obviously, there is something wrong with man's first birth. "Christ is called the second Adam. In purity and holiness, connected with God and beloved by God, *He began where the first Adam began. Willingly He passed over the ground where Adam fell, and redeemed Adam's failure.*"[4] God *must* be vindicated for creating man with a *sinless human nature*, for it was in this nature that man was overcome. The question was: Did God make a mistake in creating man, or was man responsible for his fallen condition? Never has God attempted to claim that *fallen, sinful human nature* can be victorious over Satan. If that were possible, all man would need would be an example to follow, not a Saviour who on Calvary's cross ". . . was earning the right to become the advocate of men in the Father's presence."[5] Jesus must redeem Adam's failure, then raise all men who would accept His plan of salvation by *imputing His righteousness* to them and giving them a *new nature* that God could work with, for the new nature does not hate God. This is what the new birth is all about.

"While He was free from the taint of sin, the *refined sensibilities of His holy nature* rendered contact with evil unspeakably painful to Him."[6] If Christ's nature were holy, obviously, it could not have been sinful. This could be speaking only of His human nature for its *sensibilities were refined.* In order for Christ to begin where Adam began He would, of necessity, have to have the same human nature as Adam had when He began his life here on earth. "Christ came to earth, taking humanity and standing as man's representative, to show in the controversy with Satan that man, *as God created him,* connected with the Father and the Son could obey every divine requirement."[7] He had to be tested in the "as God created him" nature that Adam was created in. The first Adam failed the testing, but the second Adam succeeded and "His holy nature" was refined.

The refining and testing process was a part of the character building that He must accomplish on man's behalf. His death then earned Him the right to impute this character to those who would believe and accept Him as Lord and Saviour.

If Jesus had a sinful nature by inheritance, how could He develop a perfect character? Paul makes it very clear that " . . . the carnal mind is enmity against God: for it is not subject to the law of God, neither indeed can be." Romans 8:7. "The brain is the capital of the body."[8] We must now discover if the brain, or mind, is also the nature of man. There is much misunderstanding in this area. A clear, penetrating statement from inspiration should help us.

> "Pure religion has to do with the will. The will is the governing power in the nature of man, bringing all the other faculties under its sway. The will is not the taste or the inclination, but it is the deciding power, which works in the children of men unto obedience to God or unto disobedience."[9]

There can be no doubt that decisions are made in the brain which is the capital of the body. We have learned that the will is the governing power, or deciding power, that works in man to obedience or disobedience. We have also learned that this will is the governing power *in the nature of man*. If we accept the governing power, or deciding power, to be the same as the brain, or mind, which is the capital of the body, we have our answer. The brain is also the residence of the nature of man. Since the heart and mind are the same, it follows that when we receive a new heart, we receive a new mind, nature and will.

As to the carnal mind Paul says, "For to be carnally minded is death; but to be spiritually minded is life and peace." Romans 8:6. Could this be the reason that David cried out in Psalm 51:10, "Create in me a clean heart, O God; and renew a right spirit within me," and Paul also counseled the Philippians, "Let this mind be in you, which was also in Christ Jesus." Philippians 2:5.

Yes, Jesus did have an advantage over sinful man, but not over the born-again Christian.

> "Through the victory of Christ the same advantages that He had are provided for man; for he may be a partaker of a power out of and above himself, even a partaker of the divine nature, by which he may overcome the corruption that is in the world through lust."[10]

The nature determines the character that will be developed. A sinful or carnal nature produces a sinful or carnal character. It can produce nothing else. "The idea that it is necessary only to develop the good that exists in man *by nature*, is a fatal deception."[11]

Now we can readily see why the new birth is essential in the experience of every man. However, Jesus needed no new birth for He was "that holy thing" or the Son of God from the beginning. Luke 1:35. *We become* sons or daughters of God through the *new birth*. We had nothing to do with our first birth, but we have everything to do with our second birth. "That which is born of the flesh is flesh; and that which is born of the Spirit is spirit." John 3:6

Character acceptable to God can only be developed in sinless nature. Jesus, the second Adam, was born with this sinless nature. We must be born *into* this sinless nature.

If the carnal mind, or nature, is ". . . not subject to the law of God . . . " Romans 8:7, and the law of God is a transcript of His character, we have a real problem if we insist that Christ inherited a sinful nature.

When Christ took upon Himself the sins of the world it did not make Him a sinner, for He did this vicariously. He took our sinful nature the same way. All the weakness and hereditary effects, physical and mental, He took so that while "sinless and exalted by nature, He consented to take the habiliments of humanity, to become one with the fallen race."[12] Habiliments, Webster defines as "characteristic apparatus." We could say identifiable characteristics.

Why is this important for us to understand? God's plan of salvation requires man to have a perfect character, and he does not have this to offer.

> "It was possible for Adam, before the fall, to form a righteous character by obedience to God's law. But he failed to do this, and because of his sin our natures are fallen and we cannot make ourselves

righteous. Since we are sinful, unholy, we cannot perfectly obey the holy law. We have no righteousness of our own with which to meet the claims of the law of God. But Christ has made a way of escape for us . . . He lived a sinless life. He died for us, and now He offers to take our sins and give us His righteousness . . . Christ's character stands in place of your character, and you are accepted before God just as if you had not sinned."[13]

This is the work of justification which is a free gift to all who will accept God's plan.

None of this would have been possible if Christ had inherited a sinful nature. But, thank God, it did happen and thus we know that "with an antagonism to evil such as can exist *only in a nature spotlessly pure,* Christ manifested toward the sinner a love which infinite goodness alone could conceive."[14]

"The humanity of Christ reached to the very depths of *human wretchedness,* and identified itself with the *weaknesses* and *necessities* of fallen man, while His *divine nature grasped the Eternal.* His work in bearing the guilt of man's transgression was not to give him license to continue to violate the law of God, which made man a debtor to the law, which debt Christ was Himself paying by His own suffering. The trials and sufferings of Christ were to impress man with a sense of his great sin in breaking the law of God, and to bring him to repentance and obedience to that law, and through obedience to acceptance with God. *His righteousness He would impute to man*, and thus raise him in moral value with God, so that his efforts to keep the divine law would be acceptable. Christ's work was to *reconcile man to God through His human nature,* and *God to man through His divine nature.*"[15]

Notice: It was through *Christ's humanity* that man was to be reconciled to God. Romans 8:7 tells us, " . . . the carnal mind [nature] is enmity against God: for it is not subject to the law of God, neither indeed can be." *Reconciliation through sinful human nature is obviously impossible*. The problem is that man has always tried to solve his sin problem by *bringing Christ down to man's own sinful nature,* rather than allowing *Christ to bring man up from his fallen, sinful nature through His imputed righteousness to stand before God with a new nature* that God can work with. The new nature does not hate God. However, man's new nature must also be refined, and this is the work sanctification accomplishes.

We can scarcely believe what the sinful nature has done to man.

> "The result of eating of the tree of knowledge of good and evil is manifest in every man's experience. There is in his nature a bent to evil, a force which, unaided, he cannot resist. To withstand this force, to attain that ideal which in his inmost soul he accepts as alone worthy, he can find no help but in one power. That power is Christ."[16]

> *"The inheritance of children is that of sin.* Sin has separated them from God. Jesus gave His life that He might unite the broken links to God. *As related to the first Adam, men receive from him nothing but guilt and the sentence of death."*[17]

In order for Christ to unite the broken links (which includes the whole human family), He must have an entirely *different nature than we are born with.*

> "Man could not atone for man. *His sinful, fallen condition* would constitute him an imperfect offering, an atoning sacrifice of less value than *Adam before his fall.* God made man perfect and upright,

and after his transgression there could be no sacrifice acceptable to God for him, unless the offering made *should in value be superior to man as he was in his state of perfection and innocency.*"[18]

The *sinful, fallen condition is sinful, fallen nature.* This is that which is passed on from generation to generation. It is this *inherited condition* that would have constituted Jesus an imperfect offering, had He *inherited sinful nature.*

Every offering selected must be without blemish of any kind. "In the days of ancient Israel the sacrifices brought to the high priest were cut open to the backbone to see if they were *sound at heart.*"[19] Jesus Christ must be pure without spot or blemish. 1 Peter 1:19. Webster defines a blemish as "an imperfection that mars or damages *immaculateness.*" It is, then, quite clear how *sinful, fallen condition, if inherited by Jesus,* would have constituted Him an imperfect offering. Hence, the offering would have to be rejected by the Father. However, *He was accepted, the atonement was perfect—without spot or blemish.*

> "The incarnation of Christ has ever been, and will ever remain a mystery. That which is revealed, is for us and for our children, but let every human being be warned from the ground of making Christ *altogether human, such a one as ourselves; for it cannot be.*"[20]

We must learn that *sinful nature* cannot be *controlled, modified* or *improved* in any way. Both the Old Testament and the New Testament teach this.

Isaiah 64:6 "But we are all as an unclean thing, and all our righteousnesses are as filthy rags . . . "

Job 14:4 "Who can bring a clean thing out of an unclean? not one."

Psalms 51:10 "Create in me a clean heart, O God; and renew a right spirit within me."

Ezekiel 36:26-7 "A new heart also will I give you, and a new spirit will I put within you: and I will take away the stony heart out of your flesh, and I will give you a heart of flesh."

John 12:24 "Verily, verily, I say unto you, Except a corn of wheat fall into the ground and die, it abideth alone: but if it die, it bringeth forth much fruit."

2 Corinthians 5:17 "Therefore if any man be in Christ, he is a new creature: old things are passed away; behold, all things are become new."

Galatians 5:24 "And they that are Christ's have crucified the flesh with the affections and lusts."

> "The Christian's life is not a modification or improvement of the old, but a *transformation of nature.* There is a *death to self and sin,* and *a new life altogether.* This change can be brought about only by the effectual working of the Holy Spirit."[21]

If we picture Christ with a *sinful nature* He would have had to undergo this same transformation. But the devil could find not even an inclination (propensity) upon which to build his temptations when tempting Christ. *This would not have been the case if Christ had inherited sinful nature.*

> "When Christ bowed His head and died, He bore the pillars of Satan's kingdom with Him to the earth. *He vanquished Satan in the same nature over which in Eden Satan obtained the victory.* The enemy was overcome by Christ in His human nature."[22]

In His human nature Christ overcame Satan. *This, sinful human nature cannot do.* It (the sinful nature) must die and be replaced, and man must be a partaker of Christ's divine nature before he can live a victorious life.

> "Be careful, exceedingly careful as to how you dwell upon the human nature of Christ. Do not set

Him before the people as a man with the propensities [inclinations] of sin. He is the second Adam.
*The first Adam was created a pure, sinless being,
without a taint of sin upon him; he was in the image of God.* He could fall, and he did fall through
transgression. Because of sin his posterity was
born with inherent propensities of disobedience.
But Jesus Christ was the only begotten [unique]
Son of God. He took upon Himself human nature,
and was tempted in all points as human nature is
tempted. He could have sinned; He could have
fallen, but not for one moment was there in Him
an evil propensity."[23]

Christ is the only child ever born with sinless human
nature. In this sense He is truly unique. Notice: Man *inherited his sinful nature.* Christ *took upon Him human nature.* "God desires to heal us, to set us free. But, since this
requires an entire transformation, *a renewing of our whole
nature*, we must yield ourselves wholly to Him."[24] Since
this is His requirement, we can understand why, "*As Jesus
was in human nature, so God means His followers to be.*"[25]
Does God mean for His follower to be hampered with fallen,
sinful nature? *What, then, was Christ's relation to our sinful human nature?*

"*He took upon His sinless nature* our *sinful nature*, that He might know how to succor those that
are tempted."[26]

There is a difference between that which Christ took upon
Himself, *through inheritance*, and *what He voluntarily took*
in order to win man back to God. He humbled Himself until
there was no lower place to which He could descend. He
became *experientially acquainted* with the weakest of the
weak. All our *infirmities, handicaps of whatever nature, He
was willing to bear*. But, we must remember Christ always
retained *His perfect hatred for sin*. If Christ had inherited a

sinful nature there would have been an *unbearable dichotomy* between *His two natures*, rather than *perfect peace*. Is that what God desires His children to have?

> "Christ could have done nothing during His earthly ministry in saving fallen man if the divine had not been blended with the human. The limited capacity of man cannot define this wonderful mystery—the blending of the two natures, the divine and the human. It can never be explained. Man must wonder and be silent. And yet man is privileged to be a partaker of the divine nature, and in this way he can to some degree enter into the mystery."[27]

Through the new birth man is freed from his old nature by death and receives a new nature by birth. It is only in this new nature that we can be a partaker of the divine nature. From the cradle to the grave there was always that perfect harmony between Christ's two natures.

Anything that man has used as an excuse for sin, Jesus was willing to bear—*abuse, loneliness, poverty, being misunderstood, family rejection, physical abuse and pain, mental torture, apparent failure in life's goals, betrayal, worked against by those closest to Him, even apparently forsaken by God Himself.* Is it any wonder that we have this counsel from God, "*We should have no misgivings in regard to the perfect sinlessness of the human nature of Christ.*"[28]

"The exact time when humanity blended with divinity, it is not necessary for us to know."[29] May I suggest something that might throw a bit of light on the subject?

> "Satan with all his synagogue—for Satan claims to be religious—determined that Christ should not carry out the counsels of heaven. After Christ was baptized, He bowed on the banks of the Jordan; and *never before had heaven listened to such a prayer as*

> *came from His divine lips. Christ took our nature
> upon Himself.* The glory of God, in the form of a
> dove of burnished gold, rested upon Him, and from
> the infinite glory was heard these words, 'This is My
> beloved Son, in whom I am well pleased.'"[30]

It is no wonder that heaven had never heard such a prayer
as came from His divine lips. If Christ at this time took the
last step in humbling Himself, just imagine what that prayer
must have been—*an earnest plea to the Father to now let
the guilt of every sin man has committed be charged against
Him.* Angels and all heavenly beings must have been
shocked beyond their capacity to understand why unwor-
thy, ungrateful, sinful man should be offered salvation *by
Christ actually taking man's guilt.* It must have been almost impossible for them to comprehend.

Adam became a sinner when he chose to believe Satan
instead of God. His *nature was changed* from a *sinless* to a
sinful nature. Christ *chose* to *take upon Himself* the guilt
of the world which included *man's sinful nature.* The cleansing process must reach *beyond the deeds of man even to the
source—the nature or mind of man. It is thus that Christ
can give us a new mind, heart or nature.* This process accomplishes *man's complete restoration* and at the same time
does not contaminate the Restorer, for the *guilt was not His
own but ours—hence vicarious and by His own choice.* Oh,
the wonder of God's plan of redemption.

When Christ entered the wilderness of temptation He
bore the heavy burden of guilt for the sins of the world.
This was a burden too great for any being less than God.
Christ was fully divine and fully human, a mystery we cannot fathom.

If Christ had a sinful human nature as an *inherited part of
Him, He could not have been the express image of His Father.* Webster defines sinful as "full of sin." He, Himself,
said, ". . . *He that hath seen me hath seen the Father . . .*"

John 14:9. (Italics supplied.)

Inherited sinful human nature can, to a limited degree, be held in control. But, is this the freedom that Christ offers the believer? How can we be delivered both from the *power* and the *penalty* of sin? *"If the Son therefore shall make you free, ye shall be free indeed."* John 8:36. (Italics supplied.)

If Christ's *perfect life of obedience* was achieved through *perfect control of His sinful nature*, then His example for us is to control *our natural sinful natures*. The Bible, however, declares *that nature* to be *incorrigible* and that *it must die, and we must be born again.* God's desire is expressed in this quotation: "He would have us comprehend something of His love in giving His Son to die that He might counteract evil, *remove the defiling stains of sin from the workmanship of God,* and reinstate the lost, elevating and ennobling the soul to its *original purity through Christ's imputed righteousness.*"[31] This imputing of His righteousness is the work He is doing now for all who truly believe. He is preparing men and women, through justification, by willingly taking the responsibility for the sins recorded against them and changing their record to read *"just as if we had never sinned."*

It would have accomplished nothing for Christ to have accepted sinful nature and even lived without sinning outwardly. The law of God convicts of sin, not only in the *act*, but in the *thought*.

> "The law of God, as presented in the Scriptures, is broad in its requirements. Every principle is holy, just, and good. The law lays men under obligation to God; it reaches to the thoughts and feelings; and it will produce conviction of sin in every one who is sensible of having transgressed its requirements. *If the law extended to the outward conduct only, men would not be guilty in their wrong thoughts, desires, and designs.* But the law requires that the

> soul itself be pure and the mind holy, that the
> thoughts and feelings may be in accordance with
> the standard of love and righteousness."[32]

The *sinful nature* constitutes the *disease of sin*, the sins
are but the *symptoms* of *the disease.* " . . . The whole head
is sick, and the whole heart faint." Isaiah 1:5. If Christ had
lived a perfect life while possessing *inherited sinful nature*, He would still be *infected with the disease* and *He
would have had to have a Saviour for Himself.*

If His nature was what kept Him from having *sinful desires*, it could not have been *sinful nature.* If He *had sinful
desires* but resisted them, it would have *contaminated Him,
for in the thought* is the seed of sin.

How can we deal with Hebrews 4:15? "For we have not
an high priest which cannot be touched with the feeling of
our infirmities; but was in all points tempted like as we are,
yet without sin."

In order to think our way through this problem it is necessary for us to set aside our preconceived ideas and try to
see sin as God sees it. *Selfishness, or self-idolatry, is the
foundation of all sin.* (See <u>Testimony Treasures</u>, vol. 1, p.
518 and <u>The Great Controversy</u>, p. 294.) *At this altar every
human being has worshiped.* He either *worships himself*
or *hates himself.* Jesus said, "He that loveth his life shall
lose it; and he that hateth his life in this world shall keep it
unto life eternal." John 12:25. This is the same message
Jesus gave to Nicodemus in John 3:6, "That which is born
of the flesh is flesh; and that which is born of the Spirit is
spirit." How was Christ tempted as we are, yet without
sin? If selfishness is the root of all sin, then *different sins*
are but *variations of the plant from which they grow*. It would
be true that the more *carefully self was camouflaged within
the temptation, the stronger would be the temptation.*

Now we know that ". . . God cannot be tempted with
evil . . ." James 1:13. Christ, while on earth was wholly
God and wholly man. Because Christ's human nature was

sinless, as was Adam's nature when he was created, and Christ's divine nature was God's nature, there was *complete harmony between His two natures—His human and divine.*

"Christ ever retained the utmost hatred for sin . . . "[33] He hated sin with a perfect hatred.

> "In the unregenerate heart there is love of sin and a disposition to cherish and excuse it. In the renewed heart there is hatred of sin and a determined resistance against it."[34]

> "Through an appreciation of the character of Christ, through communion with God, sin will become hateful to us."[35]

> "He [God] proposes to remove from man the offensive thing that He hates, but man must co-operate with God in the work. Sin must be given up, hated, and the righteousness of Christ must be accepted by faith. Thus will the divine co-operate with the human."[36]

How can God develop in man hatred for sin when man has a nature that hates God instead of sin? Romans 8:7. It is only accomplished by Paul's counsel in the same letter in chapter 12:2, "And be not conformed to this world: but be ye *transformed by the renewing of your mind*, that ye may prove what is that good, and acceptable, and perfect, will of God." (Italics supplied.) Then we will " . . . abhor that which is evil; cleave to that which is good." Romans 12:9.

We should be able to establish the fact that *Satan could not tempt Christ to do something He hated.* This hatred for sin was always natural with Christ. It is not natural with the human family. We are miles apart; how can we be tempted in the same way?

We must remember that it was on this point that the most powerful being who was ever created fell. Selfishness manifested itself in pride, jealousy, deceitfulness and open rebellion. Our first parents were victims of the same temptation. Eve was tempted to question why God withheld the fruit of the tree of knowledge of good and evil. This became very strong when she thought the serpent had gained his capacity to speak by eating of this fruit. "Why should I not have such wonderful fruit?" This is selfishness of the most common kind. Adam determined to share her fate, thinking his act was one of true love. He dared to hope that things could come out somehow, as long as he got what he wanted. This was pure selfishness! Remember, all of this activity was entered into while the individuals possessed *sinless natures*. It was the same with every *fallen angel*. This must be the method Satan used on Christ, as well as on man. How could he get Christ to reveal selfishness that would not look like selfishness? The answer lies in the following inspired quotations:

> "It was a difficult task for the Prince of life to carry out the plan which He had undertaken for the salvation of man, in clothing His divinity with humanity. He had received honor in the heavenly courts and was familiar with absolute power. It was as difficult for Him to keep the level of humanity as for men to rise above the low level of their depraved natures, and be partakers of the divine nature."[37]

> "To keep His glory veiled as the child of a fallen race, this was the most severe discipline to which the Prince of life could subject Himself."[38]

The divine nature He had set aside was *sinless*, perfect and familiar with absolute power. It was extremely difficult for Christ, while on earth, to keep His *natural divine nature* from showing through His new human *sinless nature*. This nature had been weakened by four thousand years of sin. When we are born again and Christ gives us a new sinless nature, it is extremely difficult for us to keep our crucified and buried *natural nature* which was *sinful, vile* and *filled with pride* from showing through *our born-again new nature*.

Satan's continuous temptations hurled at Christ throughout His human life were to *tempt Him to reveal that divine nature*. "If you are the Christ, prove it." These were the words spoken by humans, as well as by Satan, to Jesus. Never was Christ free from this temptation. His own family and closest disciples often urged Him along this line.

Rulers, priests and leaders were used by Satan to try to force Him to *take Himself out of His Father's hands and use His own power*. Jesus must, though familiar with absolute power, remain true to His chosen position, "*I can of mine own self do nothing . . .*" John 5:30. (Italics supplied.)

Satan is constantly tempting every born-again Christian, *even though he has a new nature that is compatible with God*, to reveal the *old nature that he has crucified*. He tempts us through the products of the old nature that controlled us for so long before we were born again. These products are our *bad habits and hereditary tendencies*. He knows them well, for he was the one who developed them in us. He fans the old nature into flame through circumstances and situations of his own making. He knows that *he cannot* resurrect our old crucified nature, and Christ *would never resurrect it. We are the only ones who can be tempted to do this.* It is through the old habits that we have not yet surrendered to Christ that Satan does his most efficient work as he tries to force us to reveal our old nature. If he can get us to yield to the habits of the old self-life often enough, he knows we will be more inclined to *discouragement and will give up.* It is *when we are in this condition that we take ourselves out of Christ's control* and often, *in rebellion, turn away from God.* This, no doubt, is why Christ *would not be discouraged.*

Christ was constantly tempted to do even the good things that He did by *using His own power*—as we are constantly tempted to take ourselves away from Christ and "do our own thing," whether good or bad.

Total surrender was Jesus' only safety, and so it is for us. He was, indeed, tempted in all points like as we are. Every temptation is, and always has been, a temptation to *demonstrate selfishness* in one degree or another. *Selfishness always separates from God. This is Satan's goal.*

If Christ had used His own power by His own choice He would not have been a perfect example for us to follow, thus the plan of salvation would have failed, for He would not have demonstrated perfect trust in His Father.

> "Jesus revealed no qualities, and exercised no powers, that men may not have through faith in Him. His perfect humanity is that which all His followers may possess, if they will be in subjection to God as He was."[39]

Perfect trust is what righteousness by faith is all about!

In order to inspire in man that perfect trust, God's plan of salvation establishes a relationship between the human family and divinity that will never end. "To assure us of His immutable counsel of peace, God gave His only-begotten Son to become one of the human family, forever to retain His human nature."[40]

> "The Son of God now at the Father's right hand, still pleads as man's Intercessor. *He still retains His human nature*, is still the Saviour of mankind."[41]

> " . . . He gave His only-begotten Son to come to earth, to take the nature of man, not only for the brief years of life, but to retain His nature in the heavenly courts, an *everlasting pledge* of the faithfulness of God."[42]

> "In passing from the scenes of His humiliation, *Jesus lost none of His humanity* . . . He never forgets that He is our representative, that He bears *our nature*."[43]

> "That Christ should *take human nature*, and by a

life of humiliation *elevate man* in the scale of moral worth with God: He should carry His adopted nature to the throne of God, and there present His children to the Father, to have conferred upon them an honor exceeding that conferred upon the angels,— this is the marvel of the heavenly universe, the mystery into which angels desire to look."[44]

"Christ's work was to *reconcile man to God through His human nature,* and *God to man through His divine nature.*"[45]

"God desires to heal us, to set us free. But since this requires *an entire transformation, a renewing of our whole nature*, we must yield ourselves wholly to Him."[46]

"In heaven it is said by the ministering angels: The ministry which we have been commissioned to perform we have done. We pressed back the army of evil angels. We sent brightness and light into the souls of men, quickening their memory of the love of God expressed in Jesus. Their hearts were deeply moved by a sense of the sin that crucified the Son of God. They were convicted. They saw the steps to be taken in conversion; they felt the power of the gospel; their hearts were made tender as they saw the sweetness of the love of God. They beheld the beauty of the character of Christ. But with the many it was all in vain. *They would not surrender their own habits and character.*"[47]

"Through the victory of Christ the *same advantages that He had are provided for man*; for he may be a partaker of a power out of and above himself, even a partaker of the divine nature, by which he may overcome the corruption that is in the world through lust."[48]

"*All the natural goodness of man is worthless*

> *in God's sight.* He does not take pleasure in any man who *retains his old nature,* and is *not so renewed* in knowledge and grace that he is a new man in Christ."[49]

> "He would have us comprehend something of His love in giving His Son to die that He might counteract evil, remove the defiling stains of sin from the workmanship of God, and *re-instate the lost, elevating and ennobling the soul to its original purity through Christ's imputed righteousness.*"[50]

This is the work to be accomplished in every born-again Christian through God's unspeakable gift of justification through faith.

The question that must be answered is: If Christ had a sinful human nature, is He to retain that nature throughout eternity? If not, then He had to be freed from that sinful nature sometime. When did this occur?—certainly not at Calvary! He was a perfect offering—not a flaw of any kind was in Him. If Christ had entertained an evil thought even once, He could have accomplished nothing more than any other human priest. Every human priest, by birth, had been contaminated with sinful human nature. Therefore, he must first make an offering for himself each year (Hebrews 9:7) before he could serve as a type of Christ. We can then rest assured that at the cross "He [Christ] *vanquished Satan in the same nature over which in Eden Satan obtained the victory.*"[51] That nature was, obviously, sinless human nature for that is the way Adam was created. He (Adam) was also defeated in his sinless human nature.

If Christ, at the cross, had the same human nature Adam had when he was created, He could not have sinful nature at the same time. A house divided against itself cannot stand. His sinless human nature did not, however, relieve His suffering at the cross or throughout His lifetime. He did take His sinless human nature with Him into heaven and will bear it forever, united and identified with humanity eternally.

> "Christ was not insensible to ignominy and dis-
> grace. He felt it all most bitterly. He felt it as much
> more deeply and acutely than we can feel suffering,
> as *His nature was more exalted and pure, and holy
> than that of the sinful race for whom He suffered.*"[52]

We are delivered from our sinful human nature through
the new birth experience. Christ, however, needed not to
be born again. His birth was into the same perfection Adam
was created in. Baptism for Christ was not a symbol of
death, burial and resurrection to newness of life. His was
an example for us to follow. Every human being must be
free from his sinful human nature which is "enmity against
God" (Romans 8:7) before he can be a follower of God.
This transformation Jesus did not need, for He was the second Adam.

Sinful human nature will be a thing of the past in the
new earth. To the born-again Christian, freedom from that
sinful nature—through God's plan of salvation—makes it
possible for heaven to begin here on earth. How thankful
we should be that our Saviour has identified Himself with
the human family by retaining our human nature forever.

Notes:

1   The Youth's Instructor, October 13, 1898.
2   The Review and Herald, April 5, 1906.
3   The Desire of Ages, pp. 174, 175. (Italics supplied.)
4   The SDA Bible Commentary, vol 7A, p. 650,
    The Youth's Instructor, June 2, 1898.
5   The Desire of Ages, p. 745.
6   The SDA Bible Commentary, vol. 7A, p. 655,
    The Review and Herald, November 8, 1887.
7   The SDA Bible Commentary, vol. 7A, p. 650,
    The Signs of the Times, June 9, 1898.

8   Messages to Young People, p. 236.
9   Messages to Young People, p. 151.
10 The Signs of the Times, January 16, 1896.
11 Steps to Christ, pp. 18, 19. (Italics supplied.)
12 The Signs of the Times, April 25, 1892.
13 Steps to Christ, p. 62.
14 Patriarchs and Prophets, p. 140. (Italics supplied.)
15 Selected Messages, book 1, pp. 272, 273.
    (Italics supplied.)
16 Education, p. 29.
17 Child Guidance, p. 475. (Italics supplied.)
18 The SDA Bible Commentary, vol. 7A, p. 665,
    The Spirit of Prophecy, vol. 2 (1877 ed.) pp. 9,10.
    (Italics supplied.)
19 The SDA Bible Commentary, vol. 1, p. 1110,
    Manuscript 42, 1901. (Italics supplied.)
20 The SDA Bible Commentary, vol. 5, p. 1129,
    Letter 8, 1895. (Italics supplied.)
21 The Desire of Ages, p. 172. (Italics supplied.)
22 The SDA Bible Commentary, vol. 7A, p. 651,
    The Youth's Instructor, April 25, 1901.
23 The SDA Bible Commentary, vol. 5, p. 1128,
    Letter 8, 1895. (Italics supplied.)
24 Steps to Christ, p. 43. (Italics supplied.)
25 Testimonies, vol. 8 , p. 289. (Italics supplied.)
26 Medical Ministry, p. 181. (Italics supplied.)
27 The SDA Bible Commentary, vol. 7, p. 904,
    Letter 5, 1889.
28 The SDA Bible Commentary, vol. 5, p. 1131,
    The Signs of the Times, June 9, 1898.
    (Italics supplied.)
29 The SDA Bible Commentary, vol. 5, p. 1129,
    Letter 8, 1895.
30 Temperance, p. 284. (Italics supplied.)
31 The Review and Herald, November 8, 1892.
    (Italics supplied.)

32 Selected Messages, book 1, p. 211. (Italics supplied.)
33 The SDA Bible Commentary, vol. 7, p. 904,
    The Signs of the Times, January 20, 1898.
34 The Great Controversy, p. 508.
35 The Desire of Ages, p. 668.
36 Testimonies, vol. 5, p. 632.
37 The SDA Bible Commentary, vol. 7, p. 930,
    The Review and Herald, April 1, 1875.
38 The SDA Bible Commentary, vol. 5, p. 1081,
    Letter 19, 1901.
39 The Desire of Ages, p. 664.
40 The Desire of Ages, p. 25.
41 The Signs of the Times, July 15, 1908.
    (Italics supplied.)
42 Selected Messages, book 1, p. 258. (Italics supplied.)
43 Testimonies to Ministers, p. 19. (Italics supplied.)
44 Sons and Daughters of God, p. 22. (Italics supplied.)
45 The Review and Herald, August 4, 1874.
    (Italics supplied.)
46 Steps to Christ, p. 43. (Italics supplied.)
47 Christ's Object Lessons, p. 318. (Italics supplied.)
48 Signs of the Times, January 16, 1896.
    (Italics supplied.)
49 God's Amazing Grace, p. 66, The Review and Her
    ald, August 24, 1897. (Italics supplied.)
50 The Review and Herald, November 8, 1892.
    (Italics supplied.)
51 The SDA Bible Commentary, vol 5, p. 1108,
    Questions on Doctrines, p. 651, The Youth's Instruc
    tor, April 25, 1901.
52 The Review and Herald, September 11, 1888.
    (Italics supplied.)

APPENDIX B

HUMAN

Will

Power of the Will

"Without *freedom of choice*, his [man's] obedience would not have been voluntary, but forced. There could have been no development of character." Patriarchs and Prophets, p. 49. (Italics supplied.)

"Many are inquiring, 'How am I to make the surrender of myself to God?' . . . What you need to understand is the true force of the will. *This is the governing power in the nature of man, the power of decision, or of choice.*" Steps to Christ, p. 47. (Italics supplied.)

"The will is the *governing power in the nature* of man, bringing *all the other faculties* under its sway. The will is not the taste or the inclination, but it is th*e deciding power* which works in the children of men unto obedience to God or unto disobedience." Testimonies, vol. 5, p. 513. (Italics supplied.)

Will Power

"As you confess before men and women your confidence in the Lord, additional strength is imparted to you. Determine to praise Him. *With firm determination comes increased will power*; . . . " The SDA Bible Commentary, vol. 3, p. 1143. Manuscript 116, 1902. (Italics supplied.)

"There is nothing harder for those who possess a *strong will* than to give up their own way, and submit to the judgement of others." Gospel Workers, p. 447.

Perseverance. determination, steadfastness reveal *will power* and are a blessing when used for the right purpose.

NATURE OF MAN

Human, Natural, Sinful

"When man transgressed the divine law, *his nature became evil*, and he was *in harmony*, and *not at variance, with Satan*. There exists *naturally no enmity* [hatred] between *sinful man* and the *originator of sin*. Both became evil through apostasy." The Great Controversy, p.505. (Italics supplied.)

"The word [Bible] *destroys* the *natural, earthly nature,* and imparts a new life in Christ Jesus. The Holy Spirit comes to the soul as a Comforter. By the transforming agency of His grace, the image of God is reproduced in the disciple; he becomes *a new creature*." The Desire of Ages, p. 391. (Italics supplied.)

" . . . Should they [Adam and Eve] once yield to temptation, *their nature would become so depraved* that in themselves they would have *no power*, and *no disposition*, to *resist Satan*." Patriarchs and Prophets, p. 53. (Italics supplied.)

"While Adam was *created sinless*, in the likeness of God, Seth, like Cain, *inherited* the *fallen nature* of his parents." Patriarchs and Prophets, p. 80.

"For what the law could not do, in that it was weak through the flesh,"—it could not justify man, because *in his sinful nature he could not keep the law*." Patriarchs and Prophets, p. 373. (Italics supplied.)

Human, Divine, Sinless

"As the graft receives life when united to the vine, so the sinner partakes of the *divine nature* when connected to Christ." Testimonies, vol. 4, p. 355. (Italics supplied.)

" . . . Man was formed in the likeness of God. *His nature was in harmony with the will of God*." Patriarchs and Prophets, p. 45. (Italics supplied.)

"'If a man love me,' Christ said, 'he will keep my words; and my Father will love him, and we will come unto him, and make our abode with him.' John 14:23. The spell of a stronger, a perfect mind will be over us; for we have a living connection with the source of all-enduring strength. *In our divine life we shall be brought into captivity to Jesus Christ.* We shall no longer live the common life of selfishness, but Christ will live in us." Christ's Object Lessons, p. 61. (Italics supplied.)

The term *"human nature"* can apply to either the *sinless* (before sin) nature, or the *born-again* nature. It can also apply to the *sinful nature* according to the context in which it is used.

Character

"The character is revealed, not by occasional good deeds and occasional misdeeds, but by the tendency of the habitual words and acts." Steps to Christ, pp. 57,58.

"Actions make habits, and habits, character . . . " Fundamentals of Christian Education, p. 194.

"Thus actions repeated form habits, habits form character, and by the character our destiny for time and for eternity is decided." Christ's Object Lessons, p. 356.

Justification

"If you give yourself to Him, and accept Him as your Saviour, then, sinful as your life may have been, for His sake you are accounted righteous. Christ's character stands in the place of your character, and you are accepted before God just as if you had not sinned." Steps to Christ, p. 62.

"While the sinner cannot save himself, he still has something to do to secure salvation. 'Him that cometh to Me,' says Christ, 'I will in no wise cast out.' But we must *come* to Him; and when we repent of our sins, we must believe that He accepts and pardons us. Faith is the gift of God, but the power to exercise it is ours . . . Jesus died for us because we were helpless to do this. In Him is our hope, our justification, our righteousness." Patriarchs and Prophets, p.431.

"The only way which he [the sinner] can attain to righteousness is through faith. By faith he can bring to God the merits of Christ, and the Lord places the obedience of His Son to the sinner's account. Christ's righteousness is accepted in place of man's failure, and God receives, pardons, justifies, the repentant, believing soul, treats him as though he were righteous, and loves him as He loves His Son." The SDA Bible Commentary, vol. 6, p. 1073, The Review and Herald, November 4, 1890.

Sanctification

" . . . Sanctification . . . is nothing less than a daily dying to self, and daily conformity to the will of God . . . Paul's sanctification was a constant conflict with self. Said he, 'I die daily.' His will and his desires every day conflicted with duty and the will of God. Instead of following inclination, he did the will of God, however unpleasant and crucifying to his nature." Testimonies, vol. 4, p. 299.

"Sanctification means habitual communion with God." The SDA Bible Commentary, vol. 7, p. 908, The Review and Herald, March 15, 1906.

" . . . We should consider the words of the apostle in which he appeals to his brethren, by the mercies of God, to present their bodies, 'a living sacrifice, holy, acceptable unto God.' This is true sanctification. It is not merely a theory, an emotion, or a form of words, but a living, active principle, entering into the everyday life." Counsels on Diet and Foods, pp. 164, 165.

"'Learn of Me,' says Jesus; 'for I am meek and lowly in heart: and ye shall find rest.' We are to enter the school of Christ, to learn from Him meekness and lowliness. Redemption is that process by which the soul is trained for heaven. This training means a knowledge of Christ. It means *emancipation* from ideas, habits, and practices that have been gained in the school of the prince of darkness. The soul must be delivered from all that is opposed to loyalty to God." The Desire of Ages, p. 330. (Italics supplied.)

Imputed

Webster's New College Dictionary, 1973, defines impute as *"to credit to a person* or a cause."

"Among the great mass of professed Christians, the grievous character of the transgression of the law of God is not understood. They do not realize that salvation can be obtained only through the blood of Christ, through His *imputed righteousness*, but this alone will avail to make fallen man what he should be, and exalt him to become a member of the Royal Family." The Review and Herald, November 8, 1892. (Italics supplied.)

In justification Christ's character is imputed (credited to the believer's account). Thus his standing before God is changed.

Imparted

Webster's New College Dictionary, 1973, defines impart as "to give, convey, or grant from or as if from a store."

"Christ imparts His righteousness to those who consent to let Him take away their sins. We are indebted to Christ for the grace [His character] which makes us complete in Him." The SDA Bible Commentary, vol. 7, p. 972, Manuscript 40, 1900.

"The righteousness by which we are justified is imputed; the righteousness by which we are sanctified is imparted. The first is our title to heaven, the second is our fitness for heaven." Messages to Young People, p. 35.

In sanctification Christ's character is imparted (or conveyed to the believer and becomes a part of his person). Thus his personality is changed.

Death to Self

"When self is crucified and Christ is formed within, the hope of glory, we shall reveal, in thought, word, and deed, the reality of our belief in the truth." Testimonies, vol. 7, p. 116.

"Words cannot describe the peace and joy possessed by him who takes God at His word. Trials do not disturb him, slights do not vex him. Self is crucified." Messages to Young People, p. 98.

"Knowing this, that our old man is crucified with him, that the body of sin might be destroyed, that henceforth we should not serve sin." Romans 6:6.

"Always bearing about in the body the dying of the Lord Jesus, that the life also of Jesus might be made manifest in our body. For we which live are always delivered unto death for Jesus' sake, that the life also of Jesus might be made manifest in our mortal flesh. So then death worketh in us, but life in you." 2 Corinthians 4:10-12.

Surrender

"There are some who are seeking, always seeking, for the goodly pearl. But they do not make an *entire surrender of their wrong habits.* They do not *die to self* that Christ may live in them. Therefore they do not find the precious pearl." Selected Messages, book 1, p. 399. (Italics supplied.)

"Implicit belief in Christ's word is true humility, true self-surrender." The Desire of Ages, p. 523.

"When the soul surrenders itself to Christ, *a new power takes possession of the new heart.* A change is wrought which man can never accomplish for himself. *It is a supernatural work, bringing a supernatural element into human nature.* The soul that is yielded to Christ becomes His own fortress, which He holds in a revolted world, and He intends that no authority shall be known in it but His own. A soul thus kept in possession by the heavenly agencies is impregnable to the assaults of Satan . . . . The only defense against evil is the indwelling of Christ in the heart through faith in His righteousness. Unless we become vitally connected with God, we can never resist the unhallowed effects of self-love, self-indulgence, and temptation to sin. *We may leave off many bad habits, for the time we may part company with Satan; but without a vital connection with God, through the surrender of ourselves to Him moment by moment, we shall be overcome."* The Desire of Ages, p. 324.

Surrender and death to self equal the same thing.

Born Again

"When the Spirit of God takes possession of the heart, it transforms the life. . . . *The blessing comes when by faith the soul surrenders itself to God.* Then that power which no human eye can see creates a new being in the image of God. . . . Its mystery exceeds human knowledge; yet *he who passes from death to life realizes that it is a divine reality."* The Desire of Ages, p. 173. (Italics supplied.)

"How, then, are we to be saved? 'As Moses lifted up the serpent in the wilderness,' so the Son of man has been lifted up, and everyone who has been deceived and bitten by the serpent may look and live. *'Behold the Lamb of God, which taketh away the sin of the world.'* John 1:29. The light shining from the cross reveals the love of God. His love is drawing us to Himself. If we do not resist this drawing, we shall be led to the foot of the cross in repentance for the sins that have crucified the Saviour. Then the *Spirit of God through faith produces a new life in the soul."* The Desire of Ages, pp. 175, 176. (Italics supplied.)

"'One thing thou lackest,' Jesus said. 'If thou wilt be perfect, go and sell that thou hast, and give to the poor, and thou shalt have treasure in heaven: and come and follow me.' Christ read the ruler's heart. *Only one thing he lacked, but that was a vital principle.* He needed the love of God in the soul. This lack, unless supplied, would prove fatal to him; his whole nature would become corrupted. By indulgence, selfishness would strengthen. *That he might receive the love of God, his supreme love of self must be surrendered.*" The Desire of Ages, p. 519. (Italics supplied.)

"The new birth is a rare experience in this age of the world. This is the reason why there are so many perplexities in the churches. Many, so many, who assume the name of Christ are unsanctified and unholy. They have been baptized, but they were buried alive. Self did not die, and therefore they did not rise to newness of life in Christ." The SDA Bible Commentary, vol. 6, p. 1075, Manuscript 148, 1897.

The born-again experience necessitates a complete surrender, a dying to self, before a new creature can be born by the power of God. We had no choice in the first birth, but the new birth must be by our choice.

Faith

"Faith is the only condition upon which justification can be obtained, and faith includes not only belief but trust." Selected Messages, book 1, p. 389.

Faith is taking God at His word.

APPENDIX C
GOD'S PLAN SANCTIFICATION

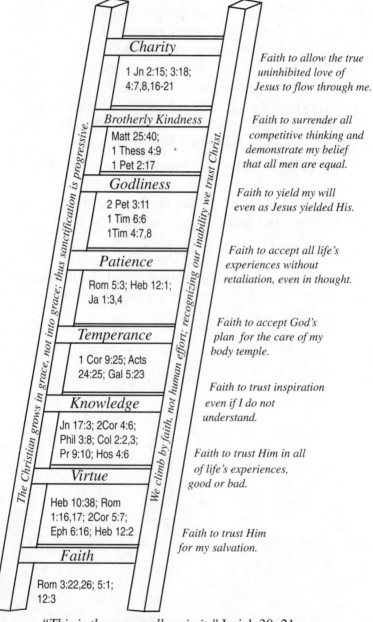

Charity

1 Jn 2:15; 3:18;
4:7,8,16-21

Faith to allow the true uninhibited love of Jesus to flow through me.

Brotherly Kindness

Matt 25:40;
1 Thess 4:9
1 Pet 2:17

Faith to surrender all competitive thinking and demonstrate my belief that all men are equal.

Godliness

2 Pet 3:11
1 Tim 6:6
1Tim 4:7,8

Faith to yield my will even as Jesus yielded His.

Patience

Rom 5:3; Heb 12:1;
Ja 1:3,4

Faith to accept all life's experiences without retaliation, even in thought.

Temperance

1 Cor 9:25; Acts
24:25; Gal 5:23

Faith to accept God's plan for the care of my body temple.

Knowledge

Jn 17:3; 2Cor 4:6;
Phil 3:8; Col 2:2,3;
Pr 9:10; Hos 4:6

Faith to trust inspiration even if I do not understand.

Faith to trust Him in all of life's experiences, good or bad.

Virtue

Heb 10:38; Rom
1:16,17; 2Cor 5:7;
Eph 6:16; Heb 12:2

Faith to trust Him for my salvation.

Faith

Rom 3:22,26; 5:1;
12:3

The Christian grows in grace, not into grace; thus sanctification is progressive.

We climb by faith, not human effort; recognizing our inability we trust Christ.

"This is the way, walk ye in it." Isaiah 30: 21

SATAN'S COUNTERFEIT PLAN

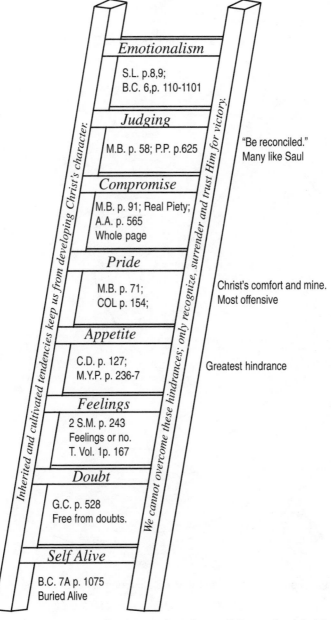

Emotionalism

S.L. p.8,9;
B.C. 6,p. 110-1101

Judging

M.B. p. 58; P.P. p.625

"Be reconciled."
Many like Saul

Compromise

M.B. p. 91; Real Piety;
A.A. p. 565
Whole page

Pride

M.B. p. 71;
COL p. 154;

Christ's comfort and mine.
Most offensive

Appetite

C.D. p. 127;
M.Y.P. p. 236-7

Greatest hindrance

Feelings

2 S.M. p. 243
Feelings or no.
T. Vol. 1p. 167

Doubt

G.C. p. 528
Free from doubts.

Self Alive

B.C. 7A p. 1075
Buried Alive

Inherited and cultivated tendencies keep us from developing Christ's character.

We cannot overcome these hindrances; only recognize, surrender and trust Him for victory.

"There is a way that seemeth right. . . ." Proverbs 16: 25

APPENDIX D
GOD WORKS FROM THE INSIDE OUT

God's Method of Imparting the Divine Nature to Man is Righteousness by Faith

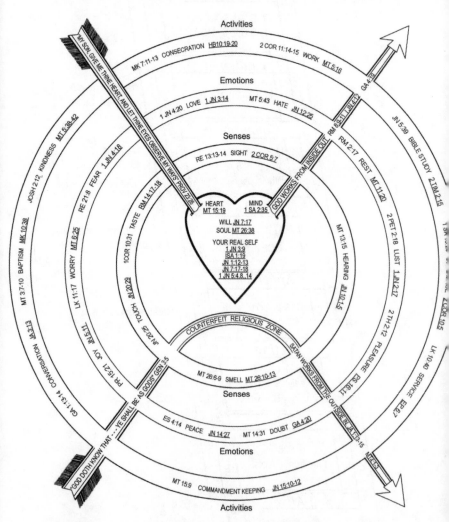

Righteousness by Works is Satan's Counterfeit of Perfecting the Human Nature

Key: Satan's Plan ----   God's Plan

HELPFUL LINKS ON THE INTERNET:

Ellen White Estate:
www.ellengwhite.org (download materials)
Hope Video Ministries
www.hopevideo.org (audio and video sermons)
David Gates:
www.gospelministries.org (sermons and books)

Justified Walk Ministries
www.justfiedwalk.com (see below)
Address and phone number (see copywrite page)
All materials are free of charge and download for free.

Other materials available from Justified Walk Ministries:
His Robe or Mine in other languages:
    Spanish, Portugese, Chinese, Malagasy
Incomplete languages available on the internet:
    Polish, Korean, French (soon)

You can find these series on the web at www.justified
walk.com. You can listen to them on-line or download them.
You can also find the associated handouts for the Justified
Walk series on-line and as downloadable pdf files. This
book, His Robe Or Mine, is also available on-line or as a
downloadable pdf file.

The Justified Walk series,
        (9 sermons on-line, CD, Cassette, MP3)
The Justified Walk handout materials, (on-line & pdf)
The Branch & The Vine series, (6 sermons on-line, CD, etc..)
Righteousness By Faith series, (10 sermons on-line, MP3)
His Robe or Mine (on-line, pdf and print)